Tula

NEW ASPECTS OF ANTIQUITY

General Editor: COLIN RENFREW

Consulting Editor for the Americas: JEREMY A. SABLOFF

RICHARD A. DIEHL

Tula

The Toltec Capital of Ancient Mexico

with 130 illustrations, 15 in color

THAMES AND HUDSON

To Clyde A. Diehl
and in memory of Helen P. Diehl

In addition to being exemplary parents, they generously
financed my first trip to Mexico, an adventure which laid the
foundation for an exciting and rewarding career.

© 1983 Thames and Hudson Ltd, London
First published in the USA in 1983 by Thames and Hudson Inc.,
500 Fifth Avenue, New York, New York 10110

Library of Congress Catalog Card Number 82–51256

Printed and bound in the German Democratic Republic

Contents

General Editor's foreword

The Toltecs of Mexico are to us a rather shadowy people – so very much more is known about their successors the Aztecs. But although the great city of the Toltecs, Tollan, was sacked around AD 1179, and many of its finest sculptures and treasures were subsequently carted away to embellish the cities of the Aztecs, its greatness lived on in memory, to be set down by the Spanish chroniclers some 350 years later when the Aztec civilization had itself, in its turn, succumbed and been swept away.

The identification of the site of Tula in the Valley of Mexico as the location of the great Toltec capital city, and the subsequent investigations there by several workers including Professor Diehl, has brought the Toltecs back into focus. We now know that their heyday extended from around AD 900 until the destruction of their principal city less than 300 years later. And we can see them more clearly now as a dominant force in Mesoamerica during that time, controlling the whole of the Valley of Mexico and extending their influence as far south as Chichen Itzá in the Maya country. We can now recognize the rise and fall of Tula as one of the decisive processes of Mexican history, to be compared with the emergence and the decline of the great city of Teotihuacan which preceded it, and indeed with the growth of the capital city of the Aztecs, now Mexico City, which came after.

All of this is of absorbing interest to anyone with any curiosity about the history and the prehistory of the Americas. But its significance is far wider. For we can see today, more clearly than we could only twenty years ago, that the paths to civilization in the New World are not unlike those followed in the great Old World heartlands such as Sumer or Egypt. We can hope to learn about each from studying the others.

Richard Diehl takes a broad approach which gives his work a wide relevance. He deals here not only with the history of the Toltecs, as it has been established from his own and earlier excavations at Tula, but with their economy, their trade, their social organization and their religion. Drawing on the results of the survey and research undertaken by other scholars, such as Eduardo Matos Moctezuma of the Instituto Nacional de Antropologia e Historia at Mexico City, and on the work of the project of the University of Missouri-Columbia, led by himself, he is able both to give a vivid account of their way of life, and to indicate those areas where future research could one day help to fill in this picture further.

We begin to understand something of the life of what was, in its day, the greatest city of Mesoamerica, covering an area of some 14 square kilometres, with a population which Professor Diehl estimates at around 30,000 inhabitants. This was comparable in scale with the greatest cities of Europe at the time – the early Middle Ages. To visit it today is an impressive experience, with its temple mounds, one of them surmounted still by great 'Atlantean' sculptures.

There remain, as Professor Diehl brings out, many tantalizing problems not yet fully solved. Where did the Toltecs come from? The legends preserved by the Aztecs give rise to conflicting opinions. And what circumstances brought about their downfall? Many factors have been suggested, but no coherent explanation has yet been put forward to account for the apparently total collapse of this great civilization. These are some of the major questions of American archaeology. The progress of prehistoric research now provides answers to some of them: others, as Professor Diehl describes, remain a challenge to the archaeologist and a spur to further work.

Colin Renfrew

Consulting Editor's foreword

The term 'Toltec' is one that is very familiar to the general public. It is often associated with a warlike, militaristic image. The Aztecs venerated their Toltec predecessors and credited them with all sorts of amazing accomplishments in the arts, politics, warfare, and other realms of life such that the Toltecs achieved a kind of legendary status. Before the beginnings of professional archaeology in the late nineteenth century, the Toltecs were even credited by some with the building of a variety of monuments not only in Mexico but throughout the eastern United States.

With the coming of modern archaeological research, knowledge of the cultural development of ancient Mexico has progressed by leaps and bounds. A host of surveys and excavations have revealed important new information, for example, about the beginnings of agriculture and settled village life, the rise of Olmec civilization of the Gulf Coast, the development of complex societies in the Valley of Oaxaca, and the spectacular growth of the great city of Teotihuacan. However, despite the pioneering archaeological and historic work of scholars such as Jorge Acosta, Wigberto Jimenez Moreno, and Henry Nicholson, until recently our knowledge about the Toltecs and their capital city of Tula was relatively limited. The extent and make-up of Tula, its economy, and the chronology of its growth were a matter of guesswork.

Such paucity of knowledge was symptomatic of a general lack of emphasis on the Postclassic period (AD 900–1521) in the archaeology of Mesoamerica (that area encompassing all or part of modern-day Mexico, Guatemala, Belize, Honduras, and El Salvador). More attention was paid to the highly visible remains of the Classic Maya, Monte Alban, or Teotihuacan. The new studies by Richard Diehl of the University of Missouri-Columbia and his associates and of Eduardo Matos Moctezuma and his colleagues from the Instituto Nacional de Antropologia e Historia have begun to rectify this imbalance at least as regards Tula and the Toltecs. The results of this new research are synthesized in an intellectually exciting and clear manner by Diehl, a highly respected scholar with wide experience in Mesoamerican archaeology, in this volume. It can only be hoped that in the foreseeable future, the popular acclaim given the ancient Toltecs will be increasingly matched by firm scientific knowledge. Certainly Professor Diehl's fine book about Tula is an important step in this direction.

Jeremy A. Sabloff

Preface

This book is about the ancient Toltecs and their capital of Tula in central Mexico. The French savant Désiré Charnay carried out the first modern archaeological excavations at Tula almost exactly one hundred years ago. Since then our knowledge of the Aztecs, Maya, Zapotecs, Olmecs, and other pre-Columbian peoples of Mexico and northern Central America, or Mesoamerica as anthropologists call it, has expanded tremendously, but studies of the Toltecs have not kept pace. Fortunately the situation has changed in recent decades and each year brings new discoveries about the Toltecs and the role they played in pre-Columbian Mesoamerica.

The University of Missouri-Columbia (UMC) Tula Archaeological Project, the focus of this book, is one of several recent research projects dealing with Toltec culture and its remains. When Professor Renfrew invited me to contribute to the New Aspects of Antiquity series, he had in mind a book emphasizing the project results. The end product contains a great deal of additional information as well; in fact, it is more a general synthesis of what we know about the Toltecs than a specifically project-oriented work. Two factors account for this change of emphasis. First, our project was a very broadly conceived attempt to study many facets of Toltec life and the very nature of the results require a broad perspective. The second reason for my approach is that I wanted to provide a book for the general public as well as my professional colleagues. I am both surprised and pleased by the number of people I meet from all walks of life who have some knowledge of the Toltecs. Their ideas are frequently incorrect, but the fault is not theirs; after all, very few books and articles have been written with them in mind. I feel a responsibility to these people. Charnay's research was supported by a wealthy patron, ours has been made possible by the taxpayers who support the University of Missouri and the National Science Foundation. They and the educated public throughout the world can legitimately expect to share in the knowledge acquired with their funds, and to have it presented in a form which does not require a PhD degree to understand it. I hope the present work at least partially discharges my responsibility in this respect.

Despite its relatively broad scope, it does not claim to be a complete compendium of Toltec life and history. Some topics are dealt with in summary fashion because we have relatively little information on them; in other cases my personal interests and biases determined the directions I took.

The UMC Tula Archaeological Project was a decade-long research program designed to study Toltec life and culture at Tula. This book is a semi-final report and interpretation of the project results, and represents the combined efforts of many people for whom I serve as spokesman. Most of them are formally acknowledged below and in the narrative text, but these are very inadequate expressions of my gratitude. Each of my collaborators has enriched our knowledge of the Toltecs and the past decade of my life and I am very grateful to all of them.

The project received financial support from the National Science Foundation (NSF) of the United States government and the University of Missouri-Columbia Research Council. The majority of the funding was provided by the NSF grants GS-2814, GS-28119, and BNS-02752; Richard Lieban, John Cornell, Nancy Gonzalez, Iwao Ishino, and John Yellen were successive directors of the NSF Anthropology Program during this time.

The field and laboratory work was carried out in Mexico under Concesiones Arqueologicas (permits) 3/70, 3/71, and 15/71 granted by the Instituto Nacional de Antropologia e Historia (INAH), a branch of the Secretaria de Educacion Publica. These permits were awarded to the University of Missouri by Agustin Yañez and Victor Bravo Ahua, directors successively of the Secretaria. Ignacio Marquina was Director of the Monumentos Prehispanicos division of INAH during the time of the fieldwork. My friend and colleague Eduardo Matos Moctezuma, then Subdirector of Monumentos Prehispanicos and Principal Investigator of the INAH Proyecto Tula, did everything he could to help our project and we would never have succeeded without his aid. The Proyecto Tula personnel helped us in many ways: particular thanks are owed to Alicia Blanco, Ana Maria Crespo, Clara Luz Diaz, Manuel Gándara, Carlos Hernandez, Guadalupe Mastache, Rene Ocaña, Alejandro Pastrana, and Juan Yadeun.

The people of Tula de Allende very graciously accepted a large and by their standards rather unorthodox group of foreigners in their midst for several summers. Their kindness and friendship made our stay a pleasant one. I particularly wish to thank Sr and Sra Mario Arguez and Don Abundio Suarez, *jefe* of the Tula Archaeological Zone, for their help in many matters large and small.

More than thirty people were involved in the fieldwork and laboratory analyses. Most were graduate or undergraduate students associated with the UMC Anthropology Department, but Harvard University, Southern Illinois University, Pennsylvania State University, and La Universidad Veracruzana were also represented. The permanent core staff included Ramon Arellanos Melgarejo, Lourdes Beauregard de Arellanos, Alice Benfer, Robert Benfer, Robert Cobean, Dan Healan, Nancy Healan, Margaret Mandeville, Terrance Stocker, James Stoutamire, Edward Stroh Jr, and Jack Wynn. Steven Armsey, Lawrence Feldman, Roger Lomas, and B. Miles Gilbert also made important contributions to the research work. I owe particularly large debts to Robert

Benfer, the Project Co-Director, and to Viola Chablé de Diehl for her unstinting support on the long road from graduate school to Tula and beyond.

Many scholars not directly associated with the project provided advice and support through the years; they include Thomas Charleton, Michael Coe, George Cowgill, David Grove, Rene Millon, Jeffrey Parsons, Mary H. Parsons, Evelyn Rattray, William Sanders, and Robert Santley. I hope they find this book useful.

Much of the information in it has been extracted from manuscripts and papers prepared for the project final reports by Alice Benfer (obsidian tools), Robert Cobean (ceramics), Lawrence Feldman (ethnohistory and molluscs), Dan Healan (architecture), Margaret Mandeville (architecture and modern ceramics), Terrance Stocker (architecture, lithics, and figurines), James Stoutamire (survey), and Edward Stroh Jr (lithics). In addition to permitting me access to their manuscripts, they discussed with me many of the interpetations presented here. I have tried to separate my ideas from theirs by using both the first person singular and plural in the text, but have not succeeded in every case. The book is as much theirs as mine. Some of my ideas are still tentative and may change by the time we publish our scholarly final reports, but I doubt that the changes will be major.

Robert Cobean, Beverly Clark, Richard A. Diehl Jr, Dan Healan, Guadalupe Mastache, Teresita Majewski and Jeremy Sabloff have read the entire manuscript and parts of it were reviewed by Margaret Mandeville, Terrance Stocker, and Phil C. Weigand. Since I have not always taken their advice the burden of errors is mine rather than theirs. Both the prospective reader and I are indebted to my fifteen-year-old son Richie. In addition to sharing the Tula experience with his mother and me as a young child, he provided me with constant encouragement while I wrote the book and also read the manuscript from the critical perspective of a non-archaeologist.

Luz Wilson typed innumerable drafts of each chapter with her usual good humor and Susan Vale, Eric Voigt, and Dan Healan prepared the final versions of the drawings. Michael O'Brien and Michael Coe also provided help with the illustrations.

Finally I wish to thank Colin Renfrew and the Thames and Hudson staff for their support and encouragement. I am grateful to them for the opportunity they so generously provided and for their forbearance as well as their help.

Following current convention, all radiocarbon dates not corrected to true calendar dates according to the bristlecone-pine calibration of radiocarbon are indicated by lower-case 'bc' (e.g. 2500 bc); corrected dates are given as 'BC'.

1 Introduction

Then there they [the Toltecs] went – they went to live, to dwell on the banks of a river at Xicocotitlan, now called Tula. Because verily they there resided together, they there dwelt, so also many are their traces which they produced.[1]

Mexico and Central America contain many ancient ruins, silent relics of civilizations which rose and fell long before the belated European 'discovery' of the Americas. Accounts written by Spanish colonists describe the Indian cultures of the sixteenth century, but their predecessors are only known through histories or legends such as the one with which this chapter opens, and modern archaeological investigations.

This book deals with one of these older civilizations, the Toltecs of central Mexico, who flourished between the ninth and thirteenth centuries of our era. Their capital was Tollan, 'Place of the Reeds' in the Nahuatl Indian language of central Mexico, located in the modern Mexican state of Hidalgo north of Mexico City. Today the archaeological site is called Tula, a corruption of the sixteenth-century name.

The Toltecs were not the oldest civilization nor was Tula the largest city in Mesoamerica, the zone of ancient high cultures which extended from central Mexico to Central America; nevertheless they played a major role in the history of the area. They controlled most of central Mexico for a century or two and had a considerable impact on societies from the southwestern United States to northern Central America. They also acted as a cultural and historical bridge between Teotihuacan and the Aztecs who were conquered by Cortes and his followers.

The aim of this book is to summarize what we know about the Toltecs and Tula. We have both archaeological and historical information to draw upon, and each contributes things the other cannot. Both sources are fragmentary, but the gaps are slowly being filled as new information is gathered each year. In fact we now know many things about the Toltecs which even the Aztecs who proudly claimed Toltec heritage could not know.

The setting

A modern traveler can drive from Mexico City to Tula in less than two hours. After turning off the Mexico City-Queretaro express highway at Tepeji el Rio, a short drive brings him to Tula de Allende, a bustling town nestling in a valley at the confluence of the Tula and Rosas rivers. A sixteenth-century cathedral rises above the other buildings, elevating the sacred above the level of mundane daily life just as Toltec pyramid-based temples did a millennium ago. The green irrigated valley is·a pleasant sight after eroded hills, thorny shrubs, and a ubiquitous coat of white dust from two nearby cement factories.

A ridge towers over the town on its north flank. At first glance it looks like all the others in the area, but closer inspection reveals earth mounds, broken pottery, rock rubble from collapsed buildings, and other archaeological debris. These are the remains of ancient Tula, a city which lay in ruins long before the Franciscan friars began building the cathedral. Until the 1970s the only inhabitants of the ridge lived in Colonia el Tesoro, a settlement of peasant farmers and craftsmen clinging to the south edge of the ridge escarpment. Now housing developments for workers at Mexico's newest and largest petroleum refinery cover portions of the ancient city, and a new irrigation canal delivers water to fields formerly used as scrubby pastures. Thousands of tourists visit the ruins every week. Some are Mexicans trying to learn about their own past; others are foreigners who gradually realize that human history consists of more than Western civilization and that Columbus was the last, rather than the first, to discover America.

plates I, II

An overview of the Toltecs and Tula

Who were the Toltecs and what was their capital like one thousand years ago? Archaeology and ethnohistory (the study of documents dealing with non-Western peoples, in this case Spanish and Native accounts of the Toltecs recorded after AD 1521) provide partial answers to these questions. The Nahuatl word *Toltecatl*, which we have simplified to Toltec in English, has several meanings. It basically refers to an inhabitant of Tollan. It also means cosmopolitan as opposed to rustic, and skilled, particularly in crafts. The latter two meanings appear to be based on Aztec veneration of the earlier Toltecs defined by the first meaning, inhabitant of Tollan. Fray Bernardino de Sahagun, a sixteenth-century Franciscan missionary who systematically studied Aztec history and culture, tells us the Toltecs were 'the first who settled here in the land; who were like the inhabitants of Babylon, wise, learned, experienced.'[2] In modern archaeological parlance the term Toltec has acquired a chronological meaning, and we often speak of a 'Toltec period', that time between AD 900 and 1200 when Toltec civilization reached its peak.

The archaeological and documentary evidence indicate that the Toltecs were a multi-ethnic group made up of people from north, northwest, and central Mexico who spoke Nahuatl, Otomi, and several other languages. Physically they looked like modern Mesoamerican Indians, although they were somewhat taller than most. Sahagun's informants told him the Toltecs were taller than the Indians of his day, and modern studies of their skeletons bear this out. The explanation is that north Mexican Indians were and still are significantly taller than their central Mexican counterparts, and we know that many Toltecs migrated to Tula from the north.

The Toltecs would seem utterly strange and barbaric to a modern time-traveler dropped off in tenth-century Tula. They practiced cranial deformation by slightly flattening the soft skulls of infants in a cradleboard to conform to their own standards of beauty. Jewels, feathers, and other objects were inserted into openings pierced through their noses, cheeks, and earlobes. Ordinary men wore loin cloths and shirt-like garments; women used wrap-around skirts and perhaps blouses. Nobles dressed in elaborate animal-skin garments decorated with feathers and covered themselves with dazzling stone and metal jewelry. They worshipped deities who required human blood and sacrificial victims, fought wars with gusto, and even practiced cannibalism. Yet they also planted crops, made love, raised children, argued about the petty affairs of daily life, composed poetry, appreciated the beauty of flowers, tried to understand man's place in the universe, and worried about the future just as we do. Despite their unusual customs they were no less human than we are and their story is an integral part of the history of humanity.

The Toltec capital was a true city, in its day the largest in Mesoamerica. The desolate ridge of today was home to at least 30,000 people. Most of the inhabitants were craftsmen and other specialists who traded their products and services for food grown by farmers living in nearby villages. The Tula Grande precinct at the south edge of the ridge was the heart of the city. It consisted of several open plazas surrounded by temples, ballcourts, government administrative buildings, and palaces. This precinct housed the rulers and the gods, the two groups who made decisions affecting the daily lives of everybody in the city.

Tula Grande was surrounded by a densely settled residential zone containing thousands of single-story masonry houses with flat roofs. Approximately two-thirds of a mile north of Tula Grande lay a group of mounds called Tula Chico which served as a major civic zone early in the history of the city. A little farther north was the El Corral temple, an unusual round structure dedicated to the foreign Huastec god Ehecatl, Lord of the Wind. The area east of Tula Grande housed a multitude of craftsmen who processed obsidian, a volcanic glass, into sharp blades and other tools. The El Salitre swamp at the bottom of the ridge in this area provided reeds for basketry and mats and may have been the original inspiration for the name Tollan ('Place of the Reeds'). The fertile alluvial valley bottoms south and west of the ridge were occupied, but much of the evidence for this has been destroyed by modern settlement and agriculture.

Until a few years ago we had no evidence that Tula was laid out on a grid plan with major avenues and uniform building orientations like other Mesoamerican centers, but recent investigations by Mexican archaeologists suggest such features were indeed present. Barely visible lines oriented to the same compass bearing as the excavated buildings have been detected on stereoscopic aerial photographs and photogrammetric maps; some may be streets and others building walls, but unfortunately they have not yet been tested by excavation.

The Rio Tula flowed through the city from south to north and was joined by the tributary Rio Rosas at the base of the ridge below Tula Grande. Bridges probably spanned both streams and the settlement occupied both banks. Summer floods in exceptionally rainy years must have caused property and crop damage, but also enriched the low-lying farmland outside the city. The rivers were the main sources of household and irrigation water and provided a transportation artery for canoe traffic and downstream movement of food-stuffs, building materials, and other heavy goods.

In addition to being the largest Mesoamerican city of its time, Tula was the capital of a state some scholars refer to as an empire. This political unit was forged through a combination of alliances, conquests, and trade, it controlled most of central Mexico and may even have extended to distant Yucatan in southern Mexico.

As mentioned earlier, much of the information in this book comes from two major archaeological projects at Tula: the Projecto Tula of the Mexican Instituto Nacional de Antropologia e Historia (INAH) and the University of Missouri-Columbia (UMC) Tula Archaeological Project. The two projects have collaborated for more than a decade, and together have accomplished much more than either could have done by itself. Although much remains to be learned, the combined findings of the two teams have substantially changed our conceptions about Tula and the Toltecs. Before we discuss that information, however, we will briefly summarize Mesoamerican prehistory in order to place the Toltecs in their historical context.

2 Synopsis of Mesoamerican geography and culture history

Archaeologists have labored many years assembling a fairly detailed picture of Mesoamerican prehistory. A comprehensive overview of the topic is beyond the scope of this book and many peoples and civilizations not directly relevant to the present topic will be omitted from the discussion that follows. Readers interested in probing further may, however, find what they require in one or other of the books listed in the bibliography.

Geography

As various chapters contain frequent references to different geographical zones it seems best to define them at the outset. At the risk of oversimplification I will divide Mesoamerica into two rather broad categories, the lowlands and highlands.

The lowlands include the coastal zones and the great 'thumb' of the Yucatan peninsula which separates the Caribbean Sea from the Gulf of Mexico. In general terms the eastern lowlands are hot, humid, and covered *fig. 1* with tropical vegetation. The area facing the Gulf of Mexico includes the states of Veracruz and Tabasco, and can be divided into three subareas named after their sixteenth-century inhabitants: the Huasteca or north Gulf coast, the Totonac homeland on the central Gulf coast, and the Olmec area or south Gulf coast. The Yucatan peninsula includes the Mexican states of Campeche, Yucatan, and Quintana Roo; the Peten district of Guatemala; and Belize: this vast area is called the Maya zone because it was the homeland of Maya civilization, one of the most spectacular ever in the Americas.

The southern coast of Mesoamerica contains two very distinct zones. North and west of the Isthmus of Tehuantepec the land is mountainous and semi-arid; below that narrow waist it widens into a wet, fertile belt of volcanic soils and tropical jungle bordered with coastal lagoons. This southeast zone is called the Soconusco and was famous in ancient times as a source of cotton and cacao. Cacao (chocolate) was a luxury product used for making a highly prized drink, and the beans served as a standard of value or primitive money.

The Mesoamerican highlands consist of valleys nestling among massive volcanic and sedimentary mountain ranges. Three major zones are of concern here: the central Mexican, southern Mexican, and Guatemalan highlands. The central Mexican highlands include the Basin of Mexico, an internally drained

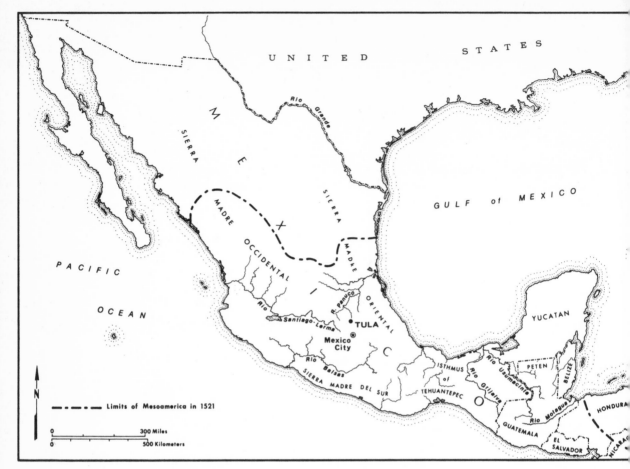

1 Map of Mexico and Northern Central America showing the approximate cultural boundaries of Mesoamerica at the Spanish Conquest.

valley which was the homeland of several important pre-Columbian civilizations and today takes in Mexico City; the valley of Toluca; Puebla; and Morelos. The southern Mexican highlands are found in the state of Oaxaca, where the Valley of Oaxaca is still occupied by Zapotec Indians whose ancestors built Monte Alban, a major city during the first millennium of our era. Continuing to the south and east we come to the highlands of Guatemala and the adjacent Mexican state of Chiapas. Although this area never produced a really major civilization, it played a very important role in Mesoamerican affairs and is still occupied by highland Maya Indians who form one of the major American Indian populations today.

Mesoamerican culture history

Mesoamerican prehistory can be divided into the seven major time periods. *Table I* This chronology is fairly new and most texts still use the older traditional

MAJOR PERIODS | TULA PHASES | COMMENTS

Date	MAJOR PERIODS			TULA PHASES	COMMENTS
1600	Spanish Colonial			Tesoro	
1500	Late Horizon	Late Post-Classic		Palacio	Aztec looting of Tula
1400	Second Intermediate	Phase Three			
1300				Fuego	
1200		Early Post-Classic		Tollan	Toltec Florescence and Collapse
1100		Phase Two			
1000					
900		Phase One		Terminal Corral	Rise of the Toltecs
800				Corral	
700				Prado	
600	Middle Horizon	Classic		Classic	Major settlement at Chingu
500					
400					
300					
200					
100	First Intermediate	Terminal Formative		Formative	First known occupation of the Tula area
AD 0 BC					
100					
200					
300		Late Formative			
400					
500					
600					
700		Middle Formative			
800					
900					
1000					
1100		Early Formative			
1200	Early Horizon				
1300					
1400					
1500					
1600	Initial Ceramic				
1700					

Table 1 Chronological chart for Mesoamerica and the Toltecs.

framework also given in Table 1 for the convenience of readers who are familiar with it.

The Lithic or Archaic Period (?–2500 bc)

This is the longest but least known timespan in Mesoamerican prehistory. Archaeologists have shown that humans first entered the Americas from northeast Asia across the now-submerged Bering Strait landbridge. The oldest presently known evidence of humans in Mesoamerica are hearths and stone tools found by Mexican archaeologists at Tlapacoya near Mexico City. These have been radiocarbon-dated to at least 20,000 years ago. Only a handful of sites are known for the period before 2000 bc, but many more will surely be found in the future.

The ways of life of these early people as reconstructed from their remains were very similar to those of the historic Teochichimeca hunters and gatherers who occupied the desert-steppe country of north Mexico at the time of the Spanish conquest. According to Sahagun, the Teochichimeca 'lived in the forests, the grassy plains, the desert, among the crags. These had their home nowhere. They only went about traveling, wandering; they went about crossing the streams, they went here and there. When night came upon them there they sought a cave, a craggy place. There they slept. . . .'[1] He went on to describe Teochichimeca food: they ate 'nopal, tuna [prickly pear leaves and fruit], roots of the *cimatl, tziuctli* cactus, honey, maguey, yucca flowers, yucca sap, maguey sap, bee honey, wild bees, wild honey, and the roots of which they had knowledge, which were in the ground; and all the meats – rabbit, snake, deer, wild animals, and all the things which flew.'[2]

The Archaic peoples, like the Teochichimeca, followed a nomadic existence, exploiting vaguely defined territories in an annual round of hunting and wild-plant collecting. The major differences were that they hunted large now-extinct mammals including mammoth, mastodon, camel, horse, and sloth; and they collected wild maize, beans, squashes, and other plants which could be domesticated. After 7000 bc, men – in fact women, for they were undoubtedly the plant collectors – began to sow and harvest these plants.

fig. 2 The best evidence for the plant domestication process has been found in dry caves in the Tehuacan valley, Puebla, where well-preserved plant remains were found. At about 7000 bc the local people collected wild grass seeds, cactus fruits and leaves, maguey hearts, and mesquite pods; they also hunted deer and cottontail rabbits now that the larger mammals were extinct. Most of the year was spent traveling in microbands composed of a few families who occupied temporary camps while they foraged in the nearby area. Several microbands coalesced into larger bands for short periods during the summer rainy seasons, when plant foods were abundant and small areas could support more people than usual.

People gradually began to domesticate some of the plants they collected; chili peppers, squash, amaranth, and avocados were domesticated first, maize

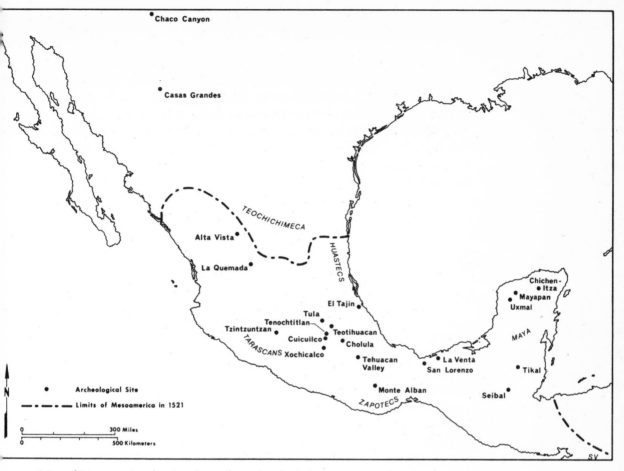

2 Map of Mesoamerica showing the major archaeological sites mentioned in the text.

and beans followed soon after. In later times maize and beans became the basic Mesoamerican staples, the base on which the civilizations were built. The domestication process was slow and several thousand years elapsed before cultivated plants replaced wild ones as the primary food source. As agriculture became more important, people settled down and spent more time living at the same place. As time went on, population growth forced them to devote more effort to farming, because wild food resources could not support the increasing numbers.

The Initial Ceramic Period (2500–1500 bc)
By 2500 bc people lived year-round in permanent villages and either invented or borrowed the idea of making pottery, perhaps from peoples in Central America or northern South America. The first ceramics were very crude, but techniques improved rapidly and pots soon became essential for cooking

and storage. Agriculture continued to grow in importance and genetic changes in the plants improved their yield.

The Early Horizon (1500–800 bc)

Small permanent villages of farming peoples were found all over Mesoamerica by 1500 bc. These basically egalitarian societies lacked social classes and specialized political, economic, and religious institutions, but such features soon appeared in some areas, marking the transition to civilized life.

Civilizations are special kinds of societies which exhibit a combination of specific traits. These include large, dense, and sedentary populations; complex social organizations; political institutions directed by the élite; and economic groups such as craft guilds and professional merchants. The central authority exerts some control over the economy and manipulates it for the benefit of the élite. It is also involved in religion and supports fulltime priests who conduct ceremonies in special shrines or temples. Some scholars add urbanism and writing to this list of attributes, but archaeology and history provide several examples of civilizations in which these were lacking.

The Early Horizon and First Intermediate Period Olmecs of the south Gulf coast were among Mesoamerica's earlier civilizations. Their centers at San Lorenzo Tenochtitlan, La Venta, Laguna de los Cerros, and Tres Zapotes were capitals of politically integrated territories and contained temples, élite residences, stone sculptures, and elaborate tombs. Their inhabitants included the rulers who directed the affairs of state, managed some sectors of the economy, provided leadership in warfare, and officiated at religious ceremonies. Hundreds of large monuments were carved on basalt blocks brought from plate 1 distant quarries. They portray secular themes glorifying the rulers and sacred representations depicting the supernatural world. The monuments also indicate a type of social organization and control not found in earlier times: moving a 40-ton piece of basalt 50 miles implies considerable planning, manpower management, and authority. In addition to the large monuments, Olmec craftsmen carved exquisite small objects from jadeite, serpentine, and other semi-precious stones imported from distant areas. The Olmec art style, Mesoamerica's earliest known artistic tradition, had a profound influence on later styles and themes.

The First Intermediate Period (800 bc–AD 300)

The Olmecs were the most precocious society of their time, but other groups in central and southern Mexico were achieving civilized status during the same period. These groups continued to flourish after the Olmec demise at about 600 bc. Intensive agriculture, sedentary village life, political organization, social classes, esoteric ritual, and elaborate art became basic characteristics of Mesoamerican life. This cultural evolution occurred earlier in the tropical lowlands than in the highlands. Many new centers emerged in the Chiapas-Guatemala coastal zone; the larger ones proudly erected stone monuments

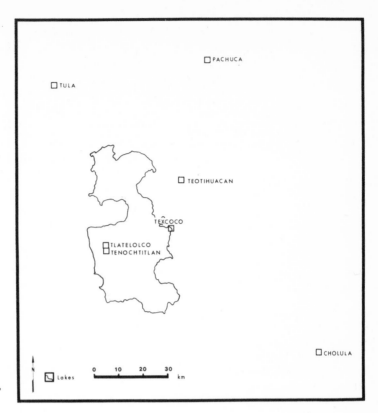

3 *Map showing the major pre-Columbian cities of central Mexico, and the Pachuca obsidian source.*

carved in the Izapa style, named after a large archaeological site near the international border. The Izapa style is significant in its own right and also provided the prototype for later lowland Classic Maya art.

Societies in the central and southern Mexican highlands developed slightly later than those in the lowlands, but by the end of the First Intermediate Period they surpassed their lowland counterparts. Certain villages grew into towns and by the end of the period we see true cities at Monte Alban, Oaxaca, and Cuicuilco and Teotihuacan in the Basin of Mexico.

The Middle Horizon (AD 300–700)
Mesoamerica was one of the few areas of the world where true cities and urban life evolved without contact from older urban societies. The Basin of Mexico centers of Cuicuilco and Teotihuacan both attained urban status a century or two before the birth of Christ. Cuicuilco appears to have been the larger of the two initially, but a lava flow covered the city and its hinterland, forcing the inhabitants to flee to Teotihuacan and elsewhere. Teotihuacan came to dominate central Mexico, and its population increased from 20,000 or 30,000 at the beginning of the Christian era to perhaps 200,000 by AD 700. Smaller cities emerged at Cholula and Monte Alban during the same period.

plate 2

fig. 3

23

Teotihuacan was the second biggest city in pre-Columbian America, the Aztec capital of Tenochtitlan alone having a larger population. It was also the direct ancestor to Tula and its collapse led to the Toltec rise. Even the Aztecs were aware of Teotihuacan's significance to their history; they believed that one of the great cycles of time and creation began there. One myth recorded in the sixteenth century states that the gods met at Teotihuacan to create the sun and moon and start the world in its present epoch:

plate 3

> When it was still night,
> When there was no day,
> When there was no light,
> They met,
> The Gods convened,
> There at Teotihuacan
> They said
> They spoke among themselves:
> 'Come here oh Gods!
> Who will take upon himself,
> Who will take charge
> of making days,
> of making light?'[3]

Teotihuacan was a truly cosmopolitan center whose inhabitants included farmers, craftsmen, priests, merchants, warriors, government officials, architects, laborers, and enclaves of resident foreigners. Most of the people lived in single-story rectangular masonry apartment houses sheltering more than 100 residents. The city was constructed on a master grid plan with the north-south axis oriented 15° 30′ east of north. Two major avenues divided it into four quadrants. The Street of the Dead, or north-south avenue, was lined with temples and other civic buildings; the east-west avenue appears to have been a more secular transportation artery.

The intersection of the two avenues was occupied by two major structures, the Ciudadela and the Great Compound. The Ciudadela was a rectangular masonry platform measuring 400 m on a side, with temples on its summit and a large interior plaza. The plaza contained the temple of Quetzalcoatl, the Feathered Serpent, one of the major Teotihuacan deities. Directly across the Street of the Dead from the Ciudadela lay the Great Compound, a low rectangular complex which may have been the principal marketplace.

plate 4

Visitors who walk north along the Street of the Dead pass a line of reconstructed temple bases extending over two-thirds of a mile, which must have presented an awe-inspiring sight when the original temples were still in place and everything was covered with polychrome murals depicting deities and mythical scenes. The vista is dominated by the Sun and Moon Pyramids, two of the largest temple mounds ever erected. The Sun Pyramid, built very early in the city's history, measures 220 m on a side and is 60 m high. A partially artificial cave excavated beneath it reflects an ancient Mesoamerican myth about ancestors and gods who emerged from caves in or under mountains, the mountain in this case represented by the Sun Pyramid itself. The somewhat smaller but no less impressive Moon Pyramid seals off the north end of the Street of the Dead.

The enormous precinct between the Moon Pyramid and the Ciudadela is impressive by day, but if one is fortunate enough to be there alone at night it is easy to imagine flickering sacred fires illuminating blood-smeared priests carrying out never-ending rituals and sacrifices. Experiences such as these make romantics out of even the most rigorously 'scientific' archaeologists!

Teotihuacan reached its peak at about AD 500, after which signs of decline began to appear. Former allies and conquered peoples broke away or were cut off from the metropolis. Farmers began to leave the city and establish new settlements near their fields; craftsmen migrated to new cities where their skills were in demand. These things indicate a weakening of Teotihuacan's government and élite, but the underlying causes are not clear. One scholar has argued that distant centers began to grow and compete effectively with Teotihuacan's merchants.[4] As the upstarts became independent, they reduced Teotihuacan's markets and prevented imports, causing unemployment and dissatisfaction in the city. This may have led to power struggles among different factions, civil war, and a general breakdown. Whatever happened, many factors appear to have been at work, each magnifying the effects of the others until the situation was beyond control.

The Second Intermediate Period (AD 700–1300)

By AD 800 Teotihuacan no longer dominated central Mexico. New communities rose and tried to emulate its former power and splendor. But only three had notable success in the period before AD 1300: Cholula, Xochicalco, and Tula. Cholula is situated east of the Basin of Mexico near modern Puebla. It was an important regional center in Teotihuacan times and remained a major community until conquered by Cortes. Xochicalco flourished in the hot, arid low country of Morelos for a few centuries during and after Teotihuacan's collapse, but was abandoned by AD 1000. Tula was only a minor village during Teotihuacan times; by AD 1000, however, it had emerged as the dominant community in central Mexico. The Toltecs extended their political and economic contacts far from their homeland and the effects of this were felt in virtually every Mesoamerican society for a brief time. Nevertheless their florescence was shortlived and Tula lay in ruins by AD 1200.

The Late Horizon (AD 1300– 1521)

Before long central Mexico experienced another phase of chaos during which many communities tried to become new Tulas. The victors were the Aztecs, who established a pan-Mesoamerican empire comparable to that of Teotihuacan. Their capital of Tenochtitlan was located a short distance south of Tula on several small islands and a man-made land surface in swampy Lake

Texcoco. Despite its seemingly unfavorable location, Tenochtitlan had between 150,000 and 300,000 inhabitants in the early sixteenth century, making it one of the world's largest cities at that time. The city in the lake elicited lavish praise from the Spaniards who conquered it. Bernal Diaz del Castillo, a battle-hardened veteran in Cortes' force, described his first impression of the Aztec capital in this manner:

During the morning, we arrived at a broad causeway, and continued our march from Ixtapalapa, and when we saw so many cities and villages built into the water and other great towns on dry land and that straight and level causeway going towards Mexico [Tenochtitlan], we were amazed and said it was like the enchantments they tell of in the legends of Amadis, on account of the great towers and cues [temples], and buildings rising from the water, and all built of masonry. And some of our soldiers asked whether the things we saw were not a dream. It is not to be wondered at that I here write it down in this manner, for there is so much to think over that I do not know how to describe it, seeing things as we did that had never been heard of or seen before, not even dreamed of.[5]

It was the Aztecs' misfortune to find themselves pitted against Spanish steel and greed in 1519, for two years later the city was a devastated rubble heap, and a culture which had taken thousands of years to evolve lay in dust and ashes.

3 Archaeological investigations at Tula

The Toltecs were never a 'lost civilization': their Aztec descendants passed on a great deal of information about them to the Spaniards after the conquest. They are the earliest Mesoamericans for whom we have abundant historical information because references to older societies are almost exclusively mythical in nature. Even the written sources dealing with the Toltecs contain as much fable as fact; for example, we are told that Toltec farmers grew multi-colored cotton and maize cobs larger than any today! Even the strictly historical accounts require cautious appraisal because pre-Columbian histories are not impartial, 'accurate' records and were often altered to support claims to noble status and dynastic legitimacy. Nevertheless ethnohistorians have begun to make sense of these confusing documents in recent years and a reasonably coherent picture is emerging.

One would expect archaeologists to be anxious to work with historically known remains of a culture like the Toltecs but in fact very little archaeology has been done at Tula and other Toltec sites. Fortunately the pace of research has increased since 1960 and should continue to do so in the future.

Previous investigations

The first excavations at Tula were done by the Aztecs in pre-Columbian times. They dug through the accumulated debris on top of abandoned buildings looking for buried offerings, carved stone decorations, and other Toltec art. Most of the excavated buildings at Tula have yielded evidence of this activity and Sahagun referred to it in the following passage: 'And Tolteca bowls, Tolteca ollas are taken from the earth. And many times Tolteca jewels – arm bands, esteemed green stones, fine turquoise, emerald green jade – are taken from the earth.'[1] Apparently most of the looted objects were reused at Tenochtitlan and elsewhere; one Toltec bench frieze found in the main precinct of the Aztec capital is now on display in Mexico's Museum of Anthropology and many other similar items undoubtedly remain to be discovered. This unscientific looting cannot be called archaeology but it certainly had a profound effect on modern investigations of the Toltecs. The Aztecs were so thorough and left Tula so impoverished that several scholars have maintained that it is not spectacular enough to have been the Toltec capital!

The first modern archaeological research at Tula was done by Désiré Charnay. This remarkable Frenchman worked under the patronage of Pierre Lorillard, a Franco-American tobacco merchant whose name is still associated with one of the giants of the industry. Charnay explored many sites in Mexico and Central America during the 1880s but Tula was a major focus of his efforts. His uncritical appraisal of the available historical documents convinced him that the Toltecs were the first civilized people in the Americas and Tula was their capital.[2] His first assumption was obviously incorrect but the second was not, even though not all are agreed on this point. While at Tula he excavated the Adoratorio, a small platform in the center of Tula Grande, and portions of two houses. His crude excavation techniques were typical of the times and on a par with Schliemann's earlier ones at Troy or of Belzoni in Egypt, but he did bring Tula to the attention of scholars and published drawings of Toltec buildings, sculptures, and artifacts.

plate 35

Almost sixty years elapsed before archaeologists returned to Tula; in the interim, investigations at Chichen Itzá and Teotihuacan recovered information relevant to Toltec studies. Colonial documents dealing with pre-Columbian Yucatan suggest that local Maya Indians were conquered by Toltecs who established their capital at Chichen Itzá. The Toltec presence at this large Maya site was demonstrated by several early scholars including John L. Stephens and Frederick Catherwood in the 1840s, Charnay in the 1880s, and Edward Thompson at the turn of the century. The Carnegie Institution of Washington began major excavations there in the 1920s under Sylvanus G. Morley, an almost legendary Maya archaeologist and epigrapher.[3] This research documented the intrusive nature of the Toltecs and revealed the defining characteristics of Toltec art and architecture. As a result archaeologists came to know more about the Toltecs in a foreign area than in their own homeland.

The Mexican archaeologist Manuel Gamio excavated the Ciudadela at Teotihuacan at about the same time. He uncovered spectacular carvings of Quetzalcoatl, the Feathered Serpent, and Tlaloc the Rain God, on the façade of the courtyard temple.[4] Toltec history and legend contain many references to the god Quetzalcoatl and Ce Acatl Topiltzin Quetzalcoatl, a priest-ruler named after him. Gamio interpreted the Ciudadela carvings as evidence that Teotihuacan had been the Toltec capital. The debate over the true location of the Toltec capital had begun before Gamio's time; some scholars felt Tula was too small and inconsequential to be the magnificent Toltec city described in the accounts, Teotihuacan's grandeur making it the obvious candidate. Gamio's evidence appeared to resolve the issue in the opinion of many, but it soon became apparent that he was incorrect.

Scholars reopened the issue of Tollan's location in the 1930s and ethnohistorian Wigberto Jimenez Moreno re-examined the evidence from a new perspective. He carefully compared modern town and place names with those associated with Tula in the historical accounts and showed that this was indeed the Toltec Tollan. The new information stimulated archaeological research at Tula, which soon proved he was correct.

Jorge R. Acosta of INAH began what turned out to be a twenty-year archaeological project at Tula in 1940. He set out to establish a chronology for the site, verify its identification as Tollan, and obtain information on Toltec culture. He excavated and partially restored Ballcourt I, the Palacio de Quetzalcoatl, Palacio Quemado, Temples B and C, the Coatepantli, and the El Corral temple.[5] He was able to establish a site chronology based on pottery style changes through time which proved that Tula was occupied after the fall of Teotihuacan. His evidence, combined with Jimenez Moreno's, clinched the case for Tula's identification as the Toltec city and provided the basis for a classic essay by Pedro Armillas establishing the archaeological-historical framework generally accepted today.[6]

The UMC Project

The beginning of the UMC Project goes back to the summer of 1961 when I visited Tula for the first time. I was a student participating in the Pennsylvania State University Teotihuacan Valley Project directed by William T. Sanders, though at that time I had no serious intention of pursuing a career in archaeology and certainly never expected to work at Tula. By the end of the summer, however, I decided that archaeology offered the most exciting prospects, and the following year I entered graduate school at Penn State, majoring in Mesoamerican archaeology and cultural anthropology under Sanders' guidance. By the time I received my PhD I had spent three additional seasons in the Teotihuacan valley and two at the Olmec site of San Lorenzo Tenochtitlan working under Michael D. Coe of Yale University. Sanders and Coe taught me many things, the most important being that archaeologists should study not only the material remains of ancient societies but also the social, economic, and political processes reflected in these remains. By doing this we can understand how the societies functioned and why they changed through time. This became the guiding principle of the Tula Project.

A second visit to Tula in 1966 suggested the need for renewed research at the site. The first serious step in this direction came in December 1969 with a reconnaissance trip to Tula accompanied by Jack T. Wynn, a UMC graduate student who later worked on the UMC Project. We spent a week covering the site on foot, taking notes, and observing the nature of the remains. The thin soil cover and scanty vegetation made the archaeological debris quite visible; the fields were littered with broken pottery, tools, and rock rubble. We soon realized that Tula had been a substantial city covering several square miles. Many research schemes came to mind, but by the time we returned home I had decided what I wanted to do and how to do it.

My basic goal was to study the daily lives of ordinary people living in the city. We knew a great deal about Toltec temples, civic buildings, and élite culture but nothing about the commoners who made up the bulk of the population. The best way to learn about this topic was through excavation of Toltec dwelling houses. Such excavations could provide information on domestic architecture, social groups, living arrangements, and routine daily activities. They would also uncover artifacts and other remains which could help refine the site chronology and shed light on Toltec economics, social organization, political structure, and household religious activities.

Three things had to be done before the project could begin; I had to find financial backing, get permission from the Mexican government to do the research, and assemble a staff. Most archaeological work done by Americans in foreign countries is supported by the National Science Foundation (NSF). I applied to the Foundation for money for a single excavation season; not only was the request granted, but the project has had its support ever since. The University of Missouri Research Council has also provided small grants at times when a few hundred dollars literally saved the day and kept the project afloat.

Archaeologists working in Mexico must have a permit from INAH, the government branch in charge of the nation's archaeological sites. I applied for a permit for the 1970 field season but my request was turned down because my plans appeared to duplicate the efforts of the INAH Proyecto Tula which was just getting underway. Whereupon the UMC Research Council quickly arranged for me to fly to Mexico City, so that I could discuss the matter with INAH officials. I met Eduardo Matos for the first time and we discussed our respective projects. He was very receptive to my ideas and we worked out an arrangement which permitted both of us to work at the site. His enthusiastic support cleared the way for my permit and the two groups have worked side by side ever since. In addition to the information we shared, we learned that science can transcend international boundaries and cultural differences. This collaboration has been one of the most pleasant and rewarding aspects of my entire Tula experience.

After the funds and permit had been secured, I began to assemble a staff. I decided to employ graduate students as crew supervisors because I strongly believe in the apprentice approach to teaching and enjoy working with students. They work hard, appreciate the opportunity to study in a foreign country – and keep me from growing old too fast! Most of the project staff came from the University of Missouri but a few were students at other institutions. The 1970 crew included Robert Cobean, Laura Flesch, Roger Lomas, Margaret Mandeville, Terrance Stocker, and Jack Wynn.

The season lasted from June until October. We did three major excavations in an area covered with dense surface debris near the north edge of the city. One was located at what we call the Corral Locality near the El Corral temple which Acosta had excavated earlier; the others were at the Canal Locality, named after a nearby abandoned irrigation canal. Mandeville took charge of the Corral Locality excavations and uncovered portions of an elaborate house.

Stocker directed one of the Canal Locality digs; instead of the house we expected to find, he uncovered a small temple platform surrounded by rooms and courtyards. Lomas and Wynn found remains of several houses facing an interior courtyard in the other section of the Canal Locality. The shallow soil in their area meant that much of the architecture had been badly disturbed by recent plowing; nevertheless they found enough to provide a good picture of Toltec houses.

While the excavations were in progress I conducted a casual survey in an attempt to locate the boundaries of the city. I used aerial photographs purchased from the Compañia Mexicana de Aerofoto, S.A. as field maps and, although only large architectural features such as mounds and terraces were visible on them, I found them of great help in finding my way about. My extremely tight schedule as Project Director compelled me to do the survey during spare moments and I did not accomplish as much as I hoped. However, I did manage to locate some of the boundaries by the end of the season. These suggested that the city covered 1.9–2.3 sq. miles (5 or 6 sq. km); later surveys more than doubled that estimate.

During my walks over the site I found an area covered with obsidian tool debris near the El Salitre swamp. It appeared to have been part of a workshop zone and we tested this idea by excavating a small pit near the end of the season. Cobean directed the excavation and found conclusive evidence that it was indeed an obsidian tool workshop.

The original project was designed to last a single season, but an unexpected turn of events drastically changed my plans: a large part of the site, I discovered, would soon suffer extensive damage. The branch of the Mexican government which deals with water resources was planning to construct an irrigation canal through the ancient residential zone. Not only were the archaeological remains along the canal right-of-way to be destroyed but the land downslope was to be leveled and graded. At least thirty percent of the ancient city would be affected, including our Canal Locality excavation area. INAH efforts to divert the canal were unsuccessful, so it was obvious that any future investigations in this area would have to be done immediately. Therefore I asked the NSF to fund two additional field seasons. The request was granted and what had started as an ordinary research project became a salvage operation competing against the bulldozers.

The project I envisaged was too large for a single person to direct and I convinced my UMC colleague Robert A. Benfer to become Project Co-Director. He is a physical anthropologist, archaeologist, and statistician who knows a great deal about computer techniques of data analysis; thus he added several dimensions to the project. The supervisory staff was also enlarged; the 1970 crew was expanded to include Ramon Arellanos Melgarejo, Lourdes Beauregard de Arellanos, Alice Benfer, Dan Healan, and James Stoutamire. The Arellanos were a husband and wife team from the Instituto Veracruzano de Antropología in Xalapa, Veracruz; the others were UMC graduate

Color plates *(pages 33–36)*

I Tula river valley. The river was an all-important source of irrigation water for the Toltecs. Jicuco mountain, seen prominently in the distance, is mentioned in sixteenth-century accounts of Tula and helped identify the site as the Toltec capital.

II Tula as seen from the west. The Tula Grande buildings occupy the ridgetop and present-day Tula de Allende can be seen at the lower right.

III Tula Grande from the southwest. Pyramid C is to the right, Pyramid B and the Vestibule to the left.

IV Pyramid B and the Vestibule at Tula Grande viewed from Pyramid C.

V Atlantean warrior columns on the summit of Pyramid B, Tula Grande. The round pieces in the foreground are sections of feathered serpent doorjambs.

VI The Palacio Quemado at Tula Grande as seen from Pyramid B. The central depressions in the floors probably coincided with the placing of skylights in the colonnaded rooms.

VII Ballcourt II, Tula Grande. View from the south looking up the central playing field of the I-shaped court.

I

II

III

VI

VII

students. A number of UMC undergraduates and people from other universities also worked during the two seasons.

We concentrated on two things in 1971 and 1972: continuation of the Canal Locality excavations and systematic surface survey of the entire ancient city. We hoped the excavations would uncover enough additional houses to enable us to define social and economic differences in the architecture and artifacts. Healan and Arellanos took charge of the excavations. Although we worked under pressure we tried to excavate as carefully as possible. Mason's trowels were the basic tools, shovels being only used for moving earth after it had been checked for artifacts. We took particular care to accurately plot the location of every unusual artifact, such as large pottery fragments, figurines, stone tools, and spindle whorls, as well as bones. We hoped this information would provide clues to the functions of rooms and other features. To a certain extent it did so, even though most of the artifacts were not in their original locations. Some were mixed in trash deposits later used as construction fill, others were discarded in abandoned rooms or on top of collapsed structures, and the locations of these objects did not tell us anything about their uses. Despite our slow rate of progress, we managed to uncover a total of fourteen houses and the temple during the three seasons, all of them in an area of about 1800 square metres.

Stoutamire directed the urban zone survey with Bob Benfer's aid. The first step was to define the entire perimeter of the city using aerial photographs as maps and ranging outward on foot from Tula Grande. When the crews found areas without archaeological remains, they continued to search for at least 300 m beyond, to be certain they had found the urban limits rather than an open space inside the city. The information was recorded on the aerial photographs and later transferred to a master map. When this task was finished we discovered that the urban limits enclosed an area of 5.4 sq. miles (14 sq. km), including the uninhabited El Salitre swamp.

The second phase of the survey involved examination of selected locations inside the city limits. Ideally we preferred to examine the entire site in detail but that would have required years and virtually unlimited funds. Since time was short and money limited, Benfer and Stoutamire worked out a sampling procedure which permitted rapid examination of small areas of the site but provided useful information about the city as a whole. A grid of squares each measuring 500 m on a side was drawn on the site map and each grid unit was subdivided into twenty-five smaller squares. Four of the twenty-five squares in each large grid unit were randomly selected for actual field examination. The survey crews then visited each selected square, took notes on the ar-chaeological remains, and collected potsherds and other artifacts from the surface. Three hundred and twenty squares (0.05 percent of the total site surface) were investigated in this fashion.

The third stage of the survey consisted of a detailed examination of strips 100 m wide along the north-south and east-west axes of the site. Artifacts were

plate XI

fig. 4

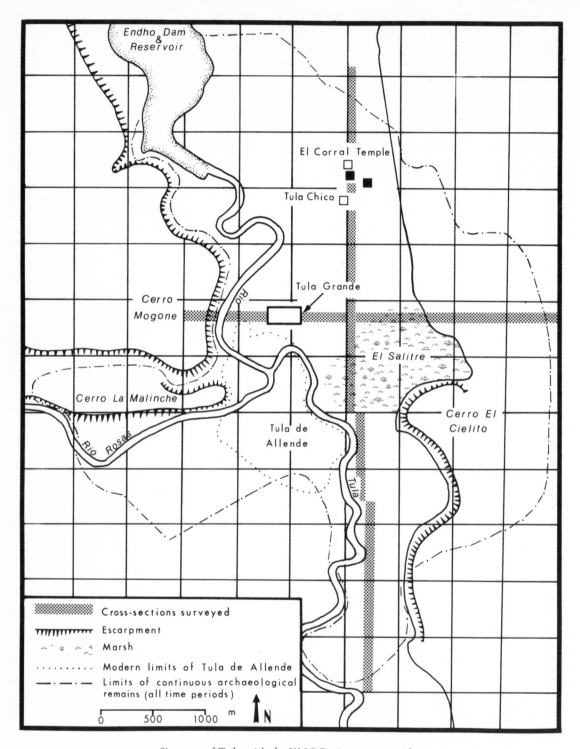

4 Site map of Tula with the UMC Project survey grid.

collected from every visible mound inside the strips and additional collections were made at 10 m intervals.

Although only a small area of the site was examined in detail, the survey provided statistically valid samples from which we may safely draw many conclusions. Surveying even this small area was a Herculean task which would not have been completed in the allotted time without the intense efforts on the part of the survey crews. Some of the crew members still jokingly refer to their former boss as 'Slavedriver Jim', and even the Mexican workers admitted that doing survey 'á la Stoutamire' was much more strenuous than excavating!

Although the excavations and surveys absorbed most of our time and energy, we were able to pursue several other research topics. Wynn prepared a topographic map of the Canal Locality area, Lawrence Feldman studied Colonial documents for clues about Toltec history and culture, Cobean carried out several small excavations and Mandeville studied modern potters who make reproductions of Toltec artifacts. Each of these activities has helped us understand the Toltecs in one way or another.

The INAH Proyecto Tula ran concurrently with ours and continued after we had finished. The major fieldwork included survey and excavations. Juan Yadeun conducted a survey of the Tula urban zone similar to ours but used different procedures. Ana Maria Crespo and Alba Guadalupe Mastache surveyed an area of 680 sq. miles (1000 sq. km) around Tula with a view to locating rural settlements and studying the history of settlement in the Toltec hinterland. Alejandro Pastrana did an intensive survey of the obsidian workshop zone at Tula and Clara Diaz studied the surface archaeology of Chingu, a large pre-Toltec center located near Tula. The major excavations included clearing and restoration of Ballcourt II by Carlos Hernandez, test pits in the Tula Chico plaza by Eduardo Matos and Robert Cobean, and excavation of a Toltec house by Augustin Peña.

By the time we had finished our fieldwork, everybody was exhausted. The last season was particularly demanding; the crews worked harder than we expected them to and all phases of the fieldwork had been more productive than we ever dared to hope. Nevertheless the project was far from complete. Two major tasks lay ahead of us: detailed studies of all the information and artifacts, and preparation of the final reports. The commonly held belief that archaeologists spend all their time excavating is a misconception. Objects must be studied, data analysed, drawings made, photographs taken, and reports written. One of my colleagues says that one month in the field requires six months of laboratory work but even this seems to me to be a gross underestimate.

While the fieldwork was in progress we attempted to do several things which would speed up the later analyses. A field laboratory was set up at the excavation site for cleaning, cataloging, and processing special finds. A larger permanent laboratory in nearby Tula de Allende processed over 200,000   plate 34 potsherds and thousands of other artifacts. Preliminary information about the artifacts was recorded directly on optical scanning sheets for computer analysis. Thus by the time the fieldwork ended we had already compiled a great deal of information on the collections for this purpose.

The analysis and report-writing phase of the project was carried out by the same students who did the fieldwork. They have incorporated much of the material into their MA theses and PhD dissertations, and revised versions of these will be published as a series of final reports. Most of the artifacts were examined in Tula de Allende because the Mexican government discourages the export of antiquities for studies which can be done in their country. The NSF and University Research Council provided funds to cover our travel, living expenses, and other costs; without these funds we could not have finished the project.

The majority of the studies were all but finished by September 1977. Then tragedy struck. One morning that year our laboratory building on the UMC campus caught fire and many field notes, photographs, manuscripts, data files, and other project documents were destroyed. Though duplicate copies of most things existed elsewhere, our computer data file took three years to reconstruct and some information was permanently lost. Whilst some evidence suggests that Tula was burned to the ground when the Toltecs finally abandoned it, the 1977 fire fortunately did not completely destroy our efforts to reconstruct their city in retrospect.

4 The Toltec beginnings

The region

The eroded hillsides, cactus thickets, and dusty air of the Tula area make one wonder why this of all places was the homeland of an ancient civilization. In reality many of these modern environmental features are the result of human activities in the past four centuries.[1] The barren surfaces and degraded vegetation can be partially attributed to overgrazing by European sheep and goats, and the foul air is a byproduct of modern cement factories which mine the same lime deposits as were exploited by the Toltecs. Although detailed information on the ancient environment is lacking, the area obviously looked much different when the Aztecs called it the Teotlalpan – 'Garden of the Gods'.

The Toltec heartland lay north of the Basin of Mexico in southern Hidalgo. Here the rivers flow northeast to join the Rio Moctezuma before it cascades down the Sierra Madre Oriental mountains to become the Rio Panuco and eventually empty into the Gulf of Mexico. The highland river valleys have always been the focal points of human occupation as they contain rich alluvial soils and irrigation water which make farming possible. Irrigation is essential because the high mountains east of Tula hold most of the clouds away from the area and summer rainfall is often insufficient for successful agriculture. Modern irrigation systems use water impounded behind dams; in ancient times temporary dams diverted water from rivers, streams, and springs into simple canals.[2] The Tula area is blessed with slightly more rain, irrigation water, and arable land than the rest of the region and thus has always been able to support more people than neighboring zones.

The climate is mild, modern average annual temperatures varying from 16 to 19 degrees C (60°–66°F) and the monthly averages from 11°C (52°F) in December to 38°C (100°F) in May.[3] Crop-killing frosts are frequent enough in winter to prevent the indigenous food plants from being grown even where irrigation water makes up for the lack of winter rain.

Modern vegetation is a greatly impoverished version of what was there when farmers first entered the area two thousand years ago. Juniper, pine and oak stands on the mountaintops are mere remnants of much more extensive ancestral forests; deforestation for timber and overgrazing have replaced them with hardy scrub and cactus thickets. Farmers cleared the valley floor vegetation long ago but some of the poorer uncultivable soils still support thorny plants such as *huizache, mesquite*, prickly pear, and yucca. The moist river banks are lined with gallery forests of willow and other tall trees which provide a verdant contrast to the otherwise stark countryside.

The pre-Columbian environment was rich in resources for human occupants; these included irrigation water, lime, wood, game, a wealth of useful wild plants, and moderate amounts of fertile land. The Toltecs utilized all these resources and began the environmental degradation which has continued ever since.

The first inhabitants

Remains of Archaic populations have been found at several places in Hidalgo but the earliest known occupation around Tula belongs to sedentary farmers who colonized the region a few centuries before the beginning of the Christian era. Mastache and Crespo's survey of the Tula region located several small First Intermediate period hamlets and villages which indicate a sparse but growing population by the end of the period.[4]

Dramatic changes occurred after AD 300. At least fifteen Middle Horizon communities were founded; Chingu, the largest, was situated adjacent to good irrigable land a few miles north of the future Tula.[5] Diaz's survey of Chingu shows it was a planned settlement which covered 1 sq. mile (2.5 sq. km). All the evidence suggests it was a regional capital established and maintained by Teotihuacan. Its rectangular house compounds and grid orientation copied these features in the latter and abundant imported Teotihuacan pottery has been found on the surface. Diaz believes that Chingu served as a collection point for locally mined lime which was exported to Teotihuacan.

Chingu's prosperity lasted for a few centuries but things took a turn for the worse after AD 600. The population declined gradually for a century and then Chingu and the other settlements in the area were abandoned. The ultimate cause must have been Teotihuacan's decline, but just what happened and where the people went is not clear. They may have moved back to Teotihuacan, to new rural settlements, or to what later became Tula.

Tula's beginning

At one time I believed that Tula was first settled between AD 700 and 750, even though others suggested a much earlier date.[6] Recent excavations in the town of Tula de Allende have proved me wrong, because First Intermediate and Middle Horizon remains were found beneath later Toltec materials.[7] We do not know how big the older communities were or if they served as a nucleus for the growth of Toltec Tula, but they do indicate that the confluence of the Tula and Rosas rivers was an important place long before the Toltecs.

The documentary and archaeological records both contain information on the founding of Tula. The documents emphasize the migration of the Toltec ancestors to Tula from other parts of Mesoamerica; some place the ancestral home on the Gulf coast, others in north Mexico. Unfortunately the accounts are so contradictory that it has been difficult to sort out history from myth. Accounts differ substantially and the same events are often attributed to different people and time periods. The picture is so confused that scholars only recently began to make sense of it after almost a century of study.[8] Among those who have been able to shed light on the problem and help clear up some of the confusion are the archaeologists.

Cobean has developed a seven-phase chronological sequence for Tula based on changes in pottery styles through time.[9] It does not include the recently discovered early materials from Tula de Allende. His first three phases precede Tula's emergence as a mature city, the fourth coincides with it, and the last three postdate its collapse. The best evidence for the three early phases was found in the Tula Chico testpits excavated by Matos and Cobean.

The Prado phase (AD 700–800)

The small quantities of Prado phase material found so far have been mixed with later remains. The vessel shapes and decorations closely resemble pottery known from elsewhere, suggesting that their makers included migrants from several regions. Some are related to a Basin of Mexico style called Coyotlatelco Red on Buff, others originally were classified as Teotihuacan imports, but more detailed studies show they were made in the Bajio zone northwest of Tula. This Bajio pottery is the first sign of the northern affiliations of at least some of the Toltecs.

The Corral phase (AD 800–900)

The Corral phase is much better known than its predecessor. Its remains have been identified at Tula Chico, Tula Grande, the Corral Locality, and several other places. This period marks the first major occupation of the Tula ridge; Yadeun calculated that the Corral phase community covered 1.2 sq. miles (3 sq. km)[10] and Stoutamire put it at 1.9 sq. miles (5 sq. km).[11] The discrepancy apparently reflects the different methodologies used in the two surveys. I favor *fig. 5* Stoutamire's figure, but regardless of who is correct, substantial growth obviously occurred during this century. The community population estimates for the period vary from 19,000 to 27,000 inhabitants; both seem excessive and until we know more about the size and spacing of Corral phase houses, I would provisionally lower them by forty or fifty percent.

The Tula Chico mound group is the only known Corral phase civic-religious complex, but structures of like age may exist beneath the later Tula Grande buildings. Although the Tula Chico mounds have not been excavated, *fig. 6* Matos' map shows that their groundplan was a duplicate of the later Tula

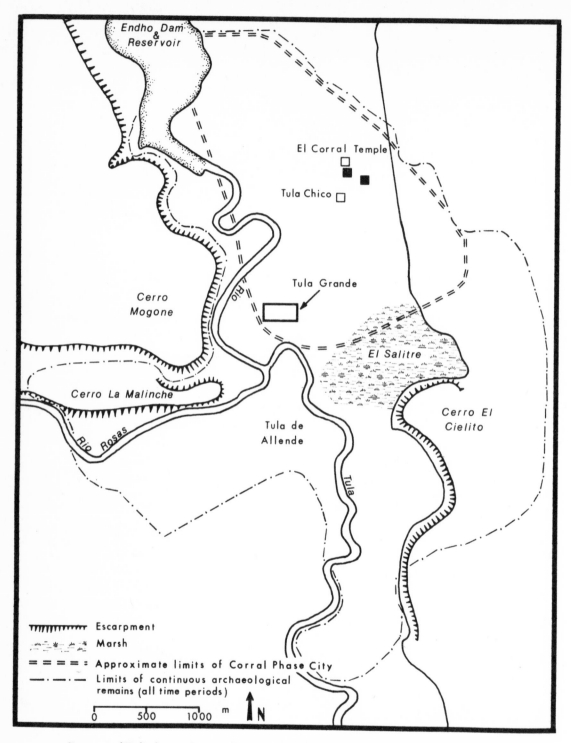

5 *Site map of Tula during the Corral phase. Black squares are UMC Project excavation areas.*

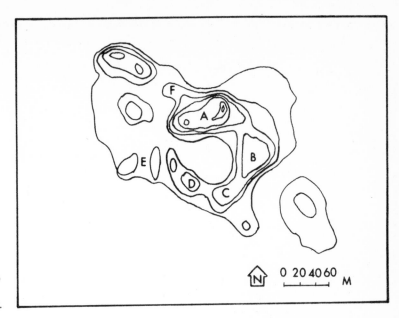

6 *Sketch of the Tula Chico mound group. Letters refer to mounds discussed in text. Contours are at 1 m intervals.*

Grande complex.[12] Analogies between the two complexes suggest that Tula Chico Mound B and the high point of Mound A functioned as temples, the low portion of Mound A was a colonnaded hall, and Mounds E and F enclosed a ballcourt. The two undesignated mounds at the northwest periphery may be another ballcourt.

The ceramics found on the surface and in the testpits at Tula Chico show the precinct was abandoned by the end of the Terminal Corral phase and remained an empty open space surrounded by dense settlement when the city was at its peak. The reason for this is a mystery but I can offer a tentative suggestion. Whereas the historical accounts contain many references to conflict at Tula, they do not clearly state who fought whom and when. The strife is frequently cast in allegorical terms as a contest between the gods Quetzalcoatl and Tezcatlipoca, and according to every account Quetzalcoatl lost and was forced to flee with his supporters. Most scholars agree that the Quetzalcoatl referred to was not the god but a priest or ruler of the same name. The encounters are traditionally dated to the time of Tula's collapse but some sources put them much earlier.

These sagas may refer to historical events involving the abandonment of Tula Chico. Both Tula Grande and Tula Chico may have served as Corral phase precincts for two different factions or ethnic groups. Conflicts between them could have resulted in the expulsion of the Tula Chico faction, perhaps including a leader named Quetzalcoatl. The winners consolidated their position and enlarged Tula Grande. They destroyed Tula Chico and left it unoccupied as a visual warning to other potential dissidents. The proscription against its use was so strict that nearby residents did not even dump rubbish containing Tollan phase sherds on it. My reconstruction may be as fanciful as the story of Quetzalcoatl's subsequent voyage across the Gulf of Mexico on a raft made of serpents, but perhaps future excavations can test it and resolve some of the enigmas surrounding the epic of Quetzalcoatl's flight.

Corral phase technology

The Corral phase pottery assemblage includes cooking pots, storage jars, tableware, and ceremonial vessels. The cooking pots were large brown basins with fire-blackened bottoms which seem well-suited for preparing beans, stews, and other watery foods. Tortillas were heated on comals, flat plates with corrugated bottoms to help conduct heat to the upper surface. Tortillas and other maize foods were prepared from dough made by cooking the kernels in lime water and grinding them on rectangular stone metates. Tortillas probably were eaten at every meal and it is difficult to overemphasize the importance of maize in the diet; in addition to being the basic source of carbohydrates, the lime-soaked maize provided the only calcium in the people's diet in the absence of domesticated milk animals. Tortillas also functioned as utensils in which to wrap and scoop up other foods.

In addition to basins and comals, culinary pottery included ladles and jars. Ladles were used to serve liquid foods. Some jars served for water and grain storage, others have lime deposits on the interior indicating the cooking of lime-impregnated maize.

Virtually all the tableware vessels were bowls with inward or outward curving walls. Some, which had three small supports forming a tripod, were probably serving dishes for liquid foods or chili-laden sauces. Bowls without supports may have functioned as hand-held eating dishes. Many bowls had elaborate decorations painted, stamped, or incised on their surfaces. The most *fig. 7* common were red painted designs in the Coyotlatelco Red on Buff style; the motifs include a bewildering array of straight and curvilinear lines, checkerboards, ellipses, crosses, dots, and other geometric elements. This popular style is a good horizon indicator, or time marker, in central Mexico and suggests widespread social ties and trade among the politically independent groups of the period. The Tula Coyotlatelco pottery is sufficiently distinct from other variants to suggest local manufacture rather than importation from elsewhere.

Ceremonial pottery vessels included 'frying pan' censers and braziers. The censers were bowls with tubular handles. They were used to burn pungent copal incense during rituals; the smoke symbolized rainclouds, and purification in copal smoke was an essential element in Mesoamerican rites. The braziers were large stationary hearths for ritual fires. Small ceramic figurines made in human and animal likenesses were probably for ritual use.

The only stone tools recovered so far in Corral phase deposits are prismatic obsidian blades struck from specially prepared cores. The obsidian workshops

7 *Coyotlatelco Red on Buff ceramic forms and motifs, of the Corral phase.*

have not been identified and we know little about the production and exchange system. Preliminary studies suggest that raw materials or finished products were imported from mining areas in the Teotihuacan valley, the state of Queretaro, and the Pachuca, Hidalgo area. The Pachuca mines became a major Toltec economic resource in later times but their significance during the Corral phase is not known. Other stone tools almost certainly included obsidian scrapers, projectile points, and bifacial knives as well as basalt manos, metates, mortars and pestles. However, these objects have not been found in the very small excavations done to date.

fig. 3

The Terminal Corral phase (AD 900–950)

The status of the Terminal Corral phase as an independent time period is uncertain because we have not found the diagnostic pottery in clearly defined, unmixed deposits and they may simply be trade wares imported near the end

8 Wavyline Mazapan Red on Buff vessel forms and designs.
Terminal Corral phase.

plate 36   of the Corral phase. The most distinctive pottery is Wavyline Mazapan Red on
fig. 8   Buff, a well-known type formerly thought to date to Tula's florescence. The
vessels are matte brown bowls and plates decorated with parallel wavy red or
purple lines applied by placing several brushes side by side in some sort of a
holder. The rarity of this pottery at Tula suggests it was imported from
somewhere in the Basin of Mexico, perhaps the Teotihuacan valley, where it
is much more common.

The Pre-Tollan phase population and its sources

The Mastache-Crespo survey shows that Tula's dramatic growth between AD
750 and 950 was accompanied by a similar expansion of the rural population.
Scores of new villages were established near good agricultural land which
could be irrigated. The majority were small settlements without civic
architecture; Tula was the largest town and functioned as the regional capital.

The rapid increase in population and changes in settlement location suggest
that substantial immigration augmented the local natural population growth.
The archaeological remains and historical sources both indicate the presence
of immigrants. These indications are fragmentary and can be interpreted in
several ways but the explanation that follows appears to make the most sense.

Archaeology, all over Mesoamerica, indicates gradual substantial population movements after AD 600. These movements appear to have involved
people from all walks of life; peasants, craftsmen, priests, and rulers. In
central Mexico most of the migrants moved short distances from Teotihuacan
to other parts of the Basin of Mexico. However, some left the Basin and
fig. 9   moved to the Tula area and elsewhere. Similar migrations at the same
time brought people southward from the northern frontier into central
Mexico. These migrations were not spectacular mass movements, nor did they
all occur at the same time. They involved small groups of perhaps a few
families or a lineage and took place intermittently over a period of several
centuries.

Nigel Davies has identified two major immigrant groups among the later
Toltecs, the Tolteca-Chichimeca and the Nonoalca.[13] The Tolteca-

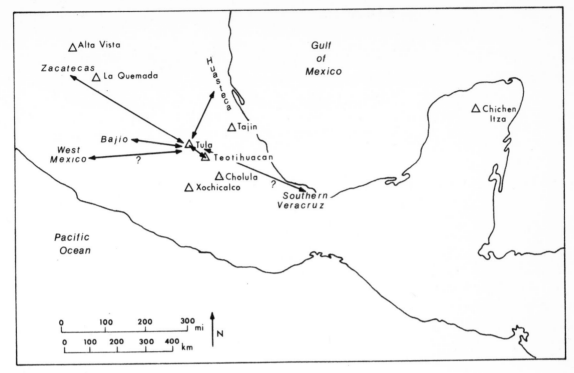

9 *Possible sources of migrants to Tula.*

Chichimeca were Nahuatl- and Otomi-speaking peasants of modest cultural attainments from the frontier zone north of Tula; the Nonoalca were highly civilized priests, merchants, and craftsmen whose place of origin is unclear. The times and precise circumstances of the migrations are likewise unclear; but, as I stated earlier, I believe they should be viewed as composite arrivals of countless small groups.

The archaeological evidence at Tula and on the northern frontier substantiates the Tolteca-Chichimeca migrations rather nicely. Investigations in the Chalchihuites area of Zacatecas and Durango[14] and the Bajio region of Queretaro, Guanajuato, and San Luis Potosi[15] show a progressive abandonment of the northern frontier by sedentary farmers after AD 600. The process followed a north to south gradient through time; the northern areas were vacated first, the southern ones somewhat later. A few of the early emigrants moved north into Durango but most apparently headed south toward the Mesoamerican core zone. Among the causes of these migrations were probably agricultural failures owing to drought, turmoil resulting from the economic impact of Teotihuacan's decline on formerly dependent mining societies in the north, as well as pressures exerted on the small northern villages by Teochichimeca nomads from the desert-steppe country to the east. There is some evidence to support each of these suggestions but, whatever the

causes, the northern frontier of agriculture and civilization did shift southward through time and the people obviously had to go somewhere.

The similarities of certain early Tula ceramics to northern wares were
mentioned earlier, and the same affinities are evident in later Tollan phase
pottery. Such resemblances can be explained in many ways but I believe they
indicate northern immigrants who continued to manufacture pottery in their
traditional ways after arriving in the Tula area. In addition to pottery styles
the northerners introduced elements such as colonnaded halls in their
architecture, death motifs in their religion, and perhaps the Tezcatlipoca cult.
All these features appear earlier at Alta Vista, Zacatecas than at Tula and
elsewhere in central Mexico.[16] The migrants probably gravitated to the Tula
area in search of land, jobs, and security. Many new characteristics of Toltec
civilization were contributed by them and, as will be seen later, they also may
have sown the seeds of Tula's destruction.

The Nonoalca are prominently mentioned in the documentary sources but
their actual identification still eludes us. Their homeland is thought to be the
lowlands of southern Veracruz and Tabasco but Davies believes they perhaps
came to Tula from Teotihuacan.[17] They are referred to as wisemen, leaders,
priests, merchants, and craftsmen; in other words, bearers of the Mesoamerican élite tradition. The sources indicate that they spoke Nahuatl, Popoloca,
Mixtec, Mazatec, and Maya. This linguistic diversity suggests that they were
not a single ethnic group but rather 'civilized people' who migrated to Tula
from almost everywhere except the northern frontier. They probably included
middle and upper class people from Teotihuacan, Monte Alban, Xochicalco,
Tajin and other centers, who were forced to search out new lives when their
home communities declined in power and importance. Tula's rising fortunes
would have attracted numerous specialists who in turn provided the growing
Toltec capital with worldly goods and spiritual benefits. The prosperity they
helped to create attracted more migrants and Tula soon became the New
Teotihuacan, later remembered as the home of those whose 'works were all
good, all perfect, all wonderful, all marvelous. . .'.[18]

Previous generations of archaeologists have been justly criticized for
invoking migration as an 'explanation' for every culture change they identified
but could not explain. Mesoamericanists in particular have been guilty of this
practice and some of their reconstructions resemble giant ethnic chess games
in which groups shoot across the landscape in ways only bishops and queens
could equal. Although in the past I have been very critical of the view that
migration was an important factor in the rise and fall of civilizations, I now
feel that it played a significant role in the case of the Toltecs. The evidence for
it is strong, and some of the factors causing the migrations can be identified.
Yet this merely locates the sources of the Toltec populations but does not
explain why Tula attracted immigrants, grew as it did, and became a major
power. Before tackling these problems, however, let us examine the Toltecs in
their peak period.

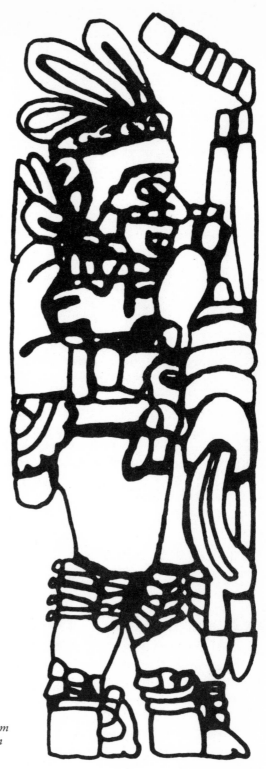

*10 Toltec warrior. Detail from
a square roof support column
on Pyramid B, Tula.*

Color plates *(pages 53–56)*

VIII Tula Grande, Pyramid B. The carved relief panels on the east façade depict jaguars and coyotes in the upper register, and below them Tlahuizcalpantecuhtli and eagles holding human hearts in their beaks.

IX Tula Grande, Palacio Quemado. Bench façade showing richly attired priests or rulers marching in single file. (Cf. plate 19.)

X This standard bearer was probably placed at the outer edge of a temple platform at Tula Grande with a banner in the hole between the hands.

XI UMC Project Canal Locality excavations in progress, 1971.

XII Chac Mool, Palacio Quemado. This is the only complete example of the seven Chac Mools known at Tula. The plate on the chest may have served as a receptacle for the hearts of sacrificial victims. Ht 66 cm.

XIII UMC Project Canal Locality excavations, 1972. House VII wall foundations are in the foreground.

XIV Plumbate drinking goblet from the House II cache, Canal Locality. Ht *c.* 10 cm.

XV Papagayo polychrome bowl from the House II cache, Canal Locality. The painted band depicts parrots. Ht *c.* 11 cm.

VIII, IX ▶

XIV

XV

5 The Tollan phase city

'And they [the Toltecs] left behind that which today is there, which is to be seen, . . . the so-called serpent column, the round stone pillar made into a serpent. Its head rests on the ground; its rattles are above. And the Tolteca mountain is to be seen; and the Tolteca pyramids, the mounds, and the surfacing of the Toltec temples.'[1]

This statement of Sahagun's and others in his work are virtually the only sixteenth-century descriptions of Toltec Tula. Fortunately archaeological investigations have revealed a great deal about the site and provide a relatively clear idea of how the city and its major buildings appeared during the Tollan phase.

Chronology

The dates for the Tollan phase (AD 950–1150) are accurate within forty or fifty years. They are based on correspondences with the Basin of Mexico sequence and historical information rather than on radiocarbon or other scientific dating techniques. Radiocarbon dating would not be of much help in trying to

Sample	UMC Project Identification Number	Date	Comments
QL 130	03409030	1020 ± 50 (A.D. 900–1000)	possible hearth or beam fragment, considered valid
QL 132	03314020	1130 ± 70 (A.D. 900–1000)	hearth, considered valid
QL 1020	0320840	1110 ± 40 (A.D. 900–1000)	possible beam fragment, considered valid
QL 1021	06050080	1070 ± 70 (A.D. 900–1000)	hearth, considered valid
QL 131	039140020	Too small	. . . .
QL 1022	06042070	360 ± 40	. . . .
QL 129	02092033	Recent	. . . .

Table II UMC Project radiocarbon determinations for the Tollan phase occupation at the Canal Locality. The bottom three are considered invalid.

Table II

determine when the phase began and ended, because dates of this age have an inherent forty to seventy year margin of error called 'the plus or minus factor'. Professor Minze Stuiver of the University of Washington dated seven radiocarbon samples from the Canal Locality which should pertain to the middle or latter part of the Tollan phase: one sample lacked sufficient carbon for accurate dating, two were contaminated with modern charcoal and yielded very recent dates, and the other four clustered between AD 900 and 1000.

We would understand the growth and decline of Tula much better if the Tollan phase were to be split up into shorter subphases; unfortunately this is not possible at the moment. Perhaps future investigators can devise a finer chronology divided into generations rather than the centuries we must work with at present.

Dates for Tula's founding and abandonment are given in the historical sources but not all scholars agree on their correlation with the Christian calendar.[2] Jimenez Moreno[3] interprets them to mean that the city was 'founded' (whatever that nebulous term may signify) in 908 and abandoned in 1156; most other interpretations differ by only a few decades.

Tula's size and population

How big was Tollan phase Tula and how many inhabitants had it? Stoutamire's survey was designed to answer these questions and yielded some very interesting information in this regard. The city covered 5.4 sq. miles (14 sq. km), including uninhabited El Salitre swamp, which occupied 0.4 sq. mile (1 sq. km). Two zones of different refuse density can be discerned; a core of 4.2 sq. miles (10.75 sq. km) with substantial surface debris from dense occup-

fig. 11

ation, and a peripheral zone of 0.9 sq. miles (2.25 sq. km) with sparse debris suggesting either dispersed houses or short-term occupation. The peripheral zone is on the south and west edges of the city and includes Tula de Allende and the surrounding irrigated farmlands. These modern features may obscure the surface remains of more intensive ancient habitation.

Yadeun's Proyecto Tula survey produced significantly different results from ours; he calculated that the Tollan phase city covered no more than 2 sq. miles (5.3 sq. km),[4] the reason being that he considers some areas within the city limits besides the El Salitre swamp to have been unoccupied, while we have evidence to the contrary. Although our results may not be one hundred percent accurate, I believe we are very close to the correct figure.

Archaeologists employ a variety of techniques for estimating the populations of ancient communities. Unfortunately these techniques are not very accurate and the larger the community, the greater the potential margin of error. One traditional method frequently used in Mesoamerica is to multiply the total occupied area by an average population density of 5000 inhabitants per sq. km. This density figure is derived from ethnographic studies of modern rural villages in the Basin of Mexico. The technique involves many dubious

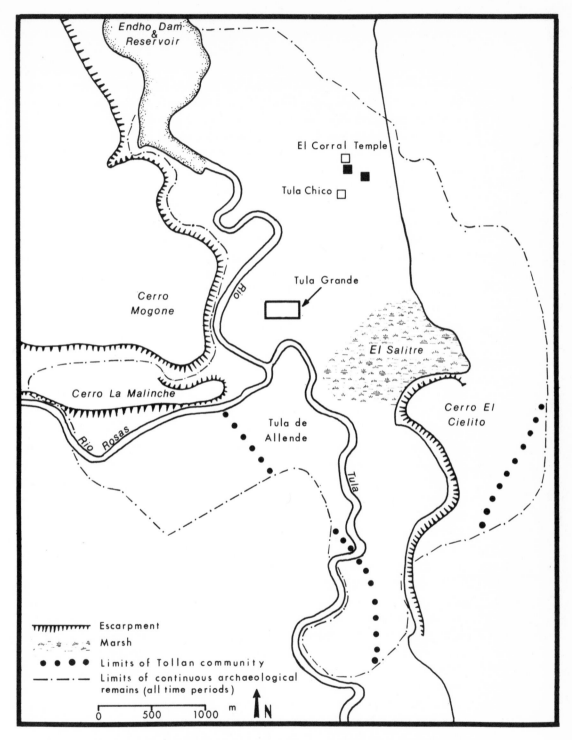

11 Map of Tula during the Tollan phase. The boundaries coincide with the limits of debris from all periods except where indicated by black dots.

Endho Dam & Reservoir

El Corral Temple

Tula Chico

Cerro Mogone

Tula Grande

El Salitre

Cerro La Malinche

Rio Rosas

Tula de Allende

Cerro El Cielito

Tula

Escarpment
Marsh
Limits of Tollan community
Limits of continuous archaeological remains (all time periods)

0   500   1000   m

N

and unproven assumptions; for example, that ancient peoples lived in the same kinds of social groups and used available space in the same manner as modern villagers. For these and other reasons, many scholars consider the technique suspect. An alternative method is to calculate the number of houses in a community and multiply it by the average number of people per house. Rene Millon used this method at Teotihuacan, where he was able to estimate the total number of dwellings based on surface survey and the average number of occupants, using data from previous excavations.[5] We cannot do this at Tula because we do not know how many houses existed or the average number of occupants.

When we began the project I believed we could estimate the city's population with a fair degree of accuracy. My optimism has diminished over the years but here, for what they are worth, are the estimates that have been made: Stoutamire calculated a Tollan phase population of 55,000 against Yadeun's estimate of 18,800–34,800. Both investigators used variants of the area-times-density method. I believe Tula's maximum population was 30,000–40,000 and that Yadeun's upper limit is near the truth, even though it is based on an inaccurate area calculation. My figure is admittedly an educated guess and I will not be surprised if it turns out to be too low.

Tula's civic architecture

plates 5, 6, 7, 8

Civic buildings have been the main focus of investigations at Tula until recently. Those excavated to date include temples, colonnaded halls, ballcourts, and similar structures. Other kinds of civic buildings one might expect to find with more excavation include palaces, marketplaces, government storehouses, and calmecacs (priestly schools).

Toltec temples took the form of a solid basal platform or mound with a small enclosed shrine at its summit. The mounds, incorrectly called pyramids, had rock and earth cores faced with carved stone tablets and stairways leading up one side. The shrines or temples proper have all been destroyed but were probably square masonry buildings with two interior rooms, an antechamber and an 'inner sanctum' where the idol was kept.

Sahagun recorded descriptions of several Tula temples.[6] According to these oral traditions, the exterior walls were covered with precious materials including gold plate, silver, coral, turquoise, red and white shells, and brightly colored feathers. The first two items seem to be a case of Aztec hyperbole but the rest may well be accurate. Each temple apparently was covered on all four walls with only one material. Unfortunately none of this has been preserved in the archaeological remains.

plate III

fig. 12
plate 9

Acosta excavated three temples; Pyramid B, Pyramid C, and the El Corral structure. Pyramid C dominated the east side of the Tula Grande precinct and was the city's largest and most important temple. The shrine, stairway, and surface of the basal mound had been completely looted and destroyed by Aztec

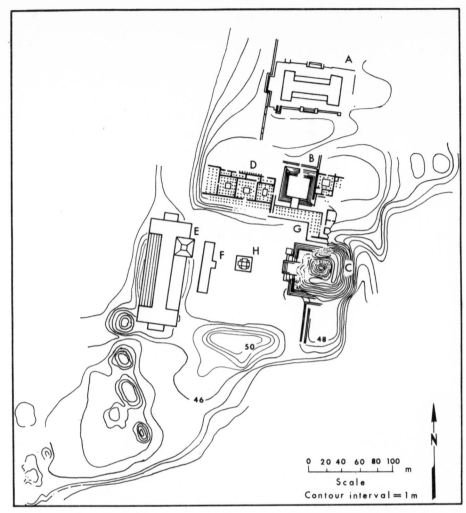

12 Ground plan of Tula Grande. A, Ballcourt I; B, Pyramid B; C, Pyramid C; D, Palacio Quemado; E, Ballcourt II; F, Tzompantli; G, Vestibule; H, Adoratorio.

vandals, who removed all the sculptures and facing stones. Although one can never be certain, I suspect this is the temple Sahagun called the Tolteca mountain in the quotation at the opening of this chapter.

Pyramid B was somewhat smaller than C; the mound measured 40 m on a side and was 10 m high. The temple and stairway faced south. Small sections of the original surface were found intact and the looters had not been able to remove all the sculptures. The intact facing stones form macabre friezes. The lower panels depict a human face emerging from the mouth of a composite monster with bird, jaguar, and serpent features who is thought to represent Tlahuizcalpantecuhtli, a form of Quetzalcoatl as Venus the Morning Star, Lord of the Dawn. Profile views of eagles and jaguars holding human hearts in

plates 10, IV

plate VIII
plates 13–16

13 *Rollout drawing of the carvings on a square shaft roof support from the summit of Pyramid B. Toltec warriors alternate with tied bundles of spears or darts.*

14 Toltec warrior. From a square roof support column on Pyramid B, Tula.

their mouths alternate with these figures. The upper frieze shows a procession of prowling jaguars and coyotes wearing necklaces or collars. There is reason to believe the animal figures represent Toltec military orders analogous to the Aztec Eagle and Jaguar Knights. The tablets may have been painted; if so, the colors have long since faded. Apparently all four sides of the mound had been decorated with identical friezes but Acosta only found a few tablets on the north and a long section on the east side. The latter were missed by the Aztec looters because they were buried under a Toltec addition to the neighboring Palacio de Quetzalcoatl.

The looters destroyed the shrine or temple when they attempted to carry off the associated sculptures. They dug a huge trench into the rear of the mound and lowered the statues down an earth ramp. For some reason they finally gave up and left some sculptures on the ramp, where they were found by Acosta. The shrine roof was supported by two types of pillars made from blocks or segments of carved basalt. One type showed Toltec warriors on all four sides of square shafts; the other portrayed a single warrior carved in the round. Acosta called the latter Atlantean figures, and they have come to symbolize Tula and Toltecs in the public's mind. The doorway into the shrine was

plates 21, 22, V
figs 10, 13, 14

15 Reconstruction drawing of the El Corral temple.

flanked by two feathered serpent or Quetzalcoatl carvings with their chins on the floor and raised tails supporting the lintel, as described by Sahagun.

plates 17, 18

A freestanding wall called the Coatepantli or Serpent Wall enclosed the north side of Pyramid B. Its north face was decorated with carved and painted tablets showing feathered serpents devouring human skeletons. These scenes are probably related to the Tlahuizcalpantecuhtli cult. The serpents formed two opposing lines which met in the center of the wall. The central scene was destroyed or removed in antiquity but almost certainly dealt with some form of Quetzalcoatl.

fig. 15

The El Corral temple, the largest outside of Tula Grande, is unusual in that the mound combines round and rectangular elements. The shrine on top was completely destroyed but in all likelihood was round with a pointed thatch roof. Central Mexican round temples were always dedicated to the Wind God Ehecatl, another of Quetzalcoatl's many guises. Numerous smaller temple mounds near El Corral seem to indicate this part of the city had special religious significance but we do not know why this was or what it involved.

plates 11, VI

The Palacio Quemado or Burnt Palace was a colonnaded hall located west of Pyramid B. The excavated portion includes three large rooms on the front or south side and several smaller ones at the back. The flat roofs were supported by round and square columns and each large room had a central

plate IX

skylight in the ceiling. Masonry benches lining the sides of two large rooms

figs 16, 17

were decorated with carved friezes depicting processions of richly dressed

plate 19

priests or dignitaries. Some of the panels still retain their original paint; the colors include red, blue, white, black and yellow. Yellow-painted jewelry

16 Relief carving of Quetzalcoatl on a bench cornice in the Palacio Quemado.

suggests gold or copper ornaments, which we know were in Mesoamerica at this time but have not been found at Tula. The processions seem to march toward the front exits and out into the vestibule between the building and the plaza, perhaps portraying actual processions which began in the building and made their way over to Pyramid B.

Acosta coined the name Palacio Quemado because he though it was a palace which was burned to the ground when Tula was abandoned. The building was undoubtedly burned, though when and from what cause we cannot tell. It seems unlikely to have been a residential palace because the layout does not resemble other Toltec houses, no kitchens have been identified, and there are not nearly enough rooms for a palace. Furthermore Acosta found caches of tobacco pipes and other ceremonial objects which suggest a non-residential function. I suspect the building served as a council hall where priests or rulers met, deliberated, and staged rituals like those shown in the friezes. The same undoubtedly was true of the Palacio de Quetzalcoatl, a second colonnaded hall Acosta partially exposed east of Pyramid B.

The two 'palaces', Pyramid B and Pyramid C, were connected by a long L-shaped platform supporting a colonnaded vestibule. Bench fragments similar to those in the Palacio Quemado were found on both sides of the Pyramid B stairway in the vestibule. Processions of carved figures march toward the stairs from two directions as if they were coming from Pyramid C and the Palacio Quemado on their way to ascend Pyramid B. The extensive use of columns as roof supports was a Toltec innovation in central Mexican architecture which allowed for larger rooms and skylight openings. The idea probably originated in north Mexico but soon spread all over Mesoamerica.

Two ballcourts have been excavated at Tula Grande; both consisted of plates 12, VII raised platforms enclosing ground level playing fields shaped like a capital I.

17 Relief carving of Mixcoatl on a bench cornice in the Palacio Quemado.

Ballplaying was an important Mesoamerican game and ritual which may have been invented by the Olmecs, although specially constructed playing fields did not become popular until after the decline of Teotihuacan. At the time of the Spanish conquest the game was played by two teams or individuals who tried to keep a solid rubber ball in play by hitting it with any part of the body except the hands and feet. Points were scored by driving the ball into the opponents' back court or through stone rings mounted high on the court's central wall. When played as a sport, the spectators engaged in frenzied betting which often turned afficionados into paupers. At times the winning team was allowed to strip spectators of their clothing and jewelry, causing some of the fastest end-of-game exits in the history of sport! When it was played as a ritual, the losers often were sacrificed and their skulls displayed on large wooden racks called *tzompantlis*. The Proyecto Tula excavated a *tzompantli* base at the east edge of Ballcourt II; the low platform which had supported the rack was littered with hundreds of human skull fragments.

plates 77, 78

A long, low rectangular building which has not been excavated occupied the south side of the Tula Grande plaza. Remains of a broad stairway are still visible on the outside, suggesting that the building was open to considerable traffic and served some important governmental function.

The center of the Tula Grande plaza contained a small platform known as the Adoratorio. Not only had the Aztecs looted it, but Charnay practically dismantled it without taking any notes. It seems too small to have supported a building and I suspect it was a large version of the courtyard altars found in Tollan phase houses. If this is true, it may have contained a high status burial of some major Toltec leader.

plates 20, 23

The Toltecs made extensive use of stone sculptures as architectural embellishment. In addition to the carved frieze panels, bench façades, and Atlantean roof supports referred to earlier, various other kinds of sculpture have been found at Tula. Unfortunately most of these pieces have not be found *in situ* and in many cases we know neither their original location nor their purpose. In some instances identical pieces discovered *in situ* at the Toltec-Maya center of Chichen Itzá provide clues as to their original functions. For example there is good evidence at the Yucatecan site that the standing figures we call standard bearers were placed atop stairways leading into temples. Also, seeing that in the Temple of the Warriors at Chichen Itzá the miniature Atlantean figures dressed as Toltec warriors with their arms above their heads supported altar tops, it seems reasonable to assume that they served the same purpose at Tula.

plate X, fig. 18

plate 25

Chac Mool sculptures are the most enigmatic class of Toltec carvings. They portray men lying in an awkward posture with their legs drawn up and heads turned on one side, each holding a plate or vessel of some sort on their chest. The plate is thought by some to be a receptacle for the hearts of sacrificial victims but this is pure speculation. Some scholars believe Chac Mools were associated with the cult of Tlaloc, the Rain God. Acosta[7] suggested that they

plate XII

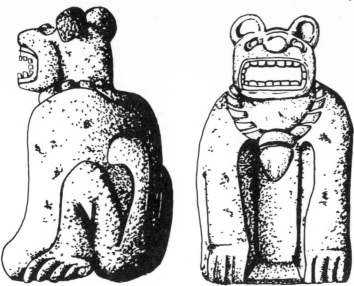

18 Two views of a carved stone jaguar standard bearer. The standard was placed in a hole behind the neck.

functioned as altars, a hypothesis which seems plausible since they have been found associated with temples at Chichen Itzá and Tenochtitlan. Whatever may be the case, six of the seven Tula examples were for some reason mutilated at the time of or after Tula's abandonment. In all cases the heads were broken off and carried away. The seventh was found in the Palacio Quemado in perfect condition.

plate 24

Toltec architecture and art are not as impressive or aesthetically pleasing as those of other ancient Mesoamericans. Tula's relatively short lifespan did not allow sufficient time for major reconstruction programs which enabled imposing architectural complexes to be built at other centers. Furthermore systematic Aztec treasure hunting removed most of the artwork, leaving an impoverished impression of what was there. Even so it is obvious the Toltecs were not not the skilled masters the Aztecs believed them to be. In Acosta's words, Toltec architecture was of 'majestic conception but mediocre execution'. Carvings were crude, mass-produced frieze elements were rapidly assembled with frequent mismatches of adjacent pieces, and basic construction techniques were not up to earlier standards.

The same generalizations apply to other Toltec craft products like pottery, figurines, and ornaments; art historians consider them shoddy compared to the works of other groups. However, beauty is in the eye of the beholder and what one person sees as crude another praises as forceful and charged with vitality. It is ironic that modern opinion, my own included, should be that Aztec art was some of the finest ever done in the Americas, while the Aztecs themselves believed Toltec works to be 'all good, all perfect, all wonderful, all marvelous. . .'.[8]

6 Toltec domestic architecture

Until recently most Mesoamerican archaeologists concentrated their efforts on temples and other spectacular remains while neglecting the houses of commoners. Whilst this one-sided approach to the study of ancient civilizations provided many insights into pre-Columbian religion and élite culture, it left us very much in the dark about everyday life. Recently however, archaeologists have begun to appreciate that ordinary house remains are a rich source of information which most of our predecessors failed to utilize.

Houses were more than mere shelters and sleeping quarters in pre-industrial societies like the Toltecs. Women and children spent most of their daily lives in or near the home and even adult males passed as much time there as anywhere else. Most of their daily activities left traces in the archaeological record, traces which help us reconstruct ancient society and understand its inner workings. House remains and the associated artifacts shed light on the technology, social organization, family life, economics and religion of ancient peoples in ways temples, palaces, and other public buildings cannot.

Our project was a pioneering attempt to study daily life in a pre-Columbian city. Previously, archaeologists had excavated a few houses at Teotihuacan and other sites but they did not try to systematically reconstruct room functions and daily activities on the basis of what they found. Thus we had very few guidelines to aid our interpretations. How could we determine who used a given room or courtyard and for what purposes? Were there any activities that left *no* traces in the archaeological record? What would indicate that occupants of one house had a higher socioeconomic status than their neighbors?

We have tried to approach these and similar problems through a combination of common sense and ethnographic analogy. Ethnographic analogies involve interpreting archaeological remains with the aid of ethnographic information on modern societies which have been studied by our colleagues in social and cultural anthropology. The analogies we used are based on information concerning the modern Mesoamerican descendents of the pre-Columbian Indian populations. Such analogies must be drawn with care because modern life differs from that of ancient times, although certain continuities do exist. For example, we know what modern peasant kitchens look like and what things they contain. When we find similar things in a Toltec room, we assume it too functioned as a kitchen. We also assume, although with somewhat less certainty, that it served the additional functions of its modern counterpart beyond being a place to prepare food. These additional functions include an informal social center for women, a 'school' where young children learn many of the basic lessons of life, and a refuge for the entire family during inclement weather. Such amenities may or may not show up in the archaeological record, but even if they do not, we are probably safe in inferring them. I suspect that many of them have in fact left traces in the archaeological remains but we lack the sophistication to understand them.

In a few instances I have ventured upon explanations of archaeological findings that cannot be positively substantiated. As a result of living among and observing people from all walks of life in Mexico for some twenty years, I have tried to discern the archaeological applications of the things to be seen in the fields and villages. These experiences and observations lie behind many of the interpretations set forth in this book.

The UMC excavations

We conducted two major excavations which exposed residential architecture; those at the Canal Locality uncovered several contiguous houses and a temple, whilst only a portion of a house was excavated at the Corral Locality. Our best information on Toltec houses comes from the Canal Locality whose remains have been analysed in detail by Dan Healan, Terrance Stocker, and Jack Wynn. In the pages that follow I have depended very heavily on Healan's study of the houses. Although we excavated only a portion of a house at the Corral Locality, Margaret Mandeville's study of the remains shows some interesting differences between them and the Canal Locality buildings. Our studies are still not completed but we do not anticipate any major changes in our final conclusions.

Healan has defined the terms 'room', 'house', and 'house group' in a very precise manner which will be followed here. Rooms are enclosed areas which were usually but not always roofed over. Houses are sets of interconnected rooms forming discrete units. House groups are clusters of houses which share an open courtyard or patio. Rooms are designated with Arabic numerals (1, 2, 3. . .), houses with roman numerals (I, II, III. . .), and house groups with directional qualifiers (East, Central, and West Group).

General characteristics of Toltec houses

Toltec houses were square or rectangular buildings containing several rooms. To the best of our knowledge, they never occurred as isolated structures but always formed a complex containing as many as five houses facing an interior courtyard. Each house group was isolated from its neighbors by a combination of exterior house walls and free-standing courtyard walls. Entry ways into house groups were peculiar L-shaped openings in the walls which Healan

plate XIII

figs 19, 20

69

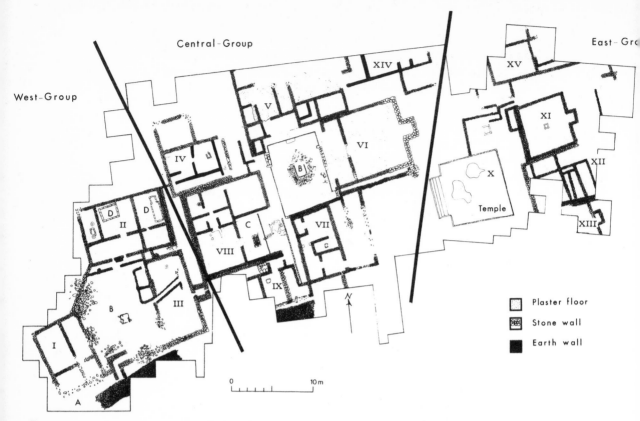

19 *Ground plan of the Canal Locality. I–IX and XI–XIV are houses; A, possible street; B, courtyard altars; C, kiln; D, subterranean storage pits.*

calls 'baffled entry ways'. This meant that one had to make two ninety-degree turns before entering the courtyard, thus insuring the privacy of the occupants from the prying eyes of outsiders on the street.

Houses were either built directly on the ground or on raised platforms. In the former case the surface was levelled or the soil stripped from the bedrock to provide a firm foundation. Raised platforms were constructed of mounded earth and rubble held in place by stone retaining walls. If older houses existed at the building site, they were razed and the floors and wall stubs incorporated into the new platform. Platform fill was obtained from nearby rubbish deposits and often contained many broken artifacts.

Stone and earth were the basic wall construction materials. Weight-bearing
plate 28 exterior walls usually had *tepetate* (a local type of limestone) block foundations laid in mud mortar. The stone apparently was quarried near the construction site; we found a quarry area near the north edge of the Canal Locality which was later used as a rubbish dump. Upper wall sections were built of sun-dried adobe blocks laid in mud mortar.

Interior room walls and partitions were constructed in various ways. Some
plate 30 were similar to exterior walls, others were made entirely of adobes, and a few

consisted of molded and compacted clay. Fine earth or lime plaster facings were placed on the interior walls in some cases, and we found evidence of paint over a plaster base in House VI. Houses were frequently modified and renovated by adding or removing walls and doorways, and although we could work out the modification sequences, the reasons for them are not always clear.

Doorways varied in size and elaborateness; some were wide passages framed with timber jambs while others were no more than narrow openings. A few interior doorways had high sills or thresholds on the floor. There is no evidence for permanent doors, but mats or cloth hangings may have provided privacy and protection from the elements.

We believe the roofs were flat surfaces similar to Aztec house roofs as described by the Spaniards, but we did not find any debris to suggest the construction materials. In some cases cylindrical or conical ceramic tubes were   plate 29 placed at the roof edges to drain off rainwater.

Most floors had surfaces of clay or earth which may have been level when new but were soon worn down unevenly through use. Some rooms had lime plaster floors which proved much more durable than the plaster wall facings. The rooms with plastered walls and floors were in the main large ones containing unusual artifacts, suggesting that the occupants had higher status or greater wealth than most other people.

Evidence of architectural embellishment was lacking in most of the structures we examined, though there were a few exceptions. The rubble

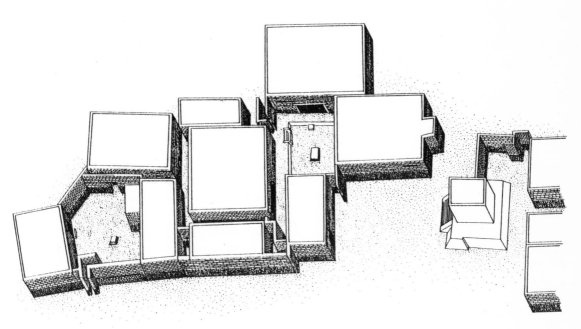

20 Reconstruction drawing of the Canal Locality structures. All are houses except for the temple structure on the right (X in fig. 19).

DMH

around Houses V and VI included several fragments of *almenas*, carved stone ornaments placed around the tops of house walls. Unfortunately they are all too incomplete to determine their original shape. House VII apparently had a carved stone band or frieze built into the upper part of the wall facing on to the Central Group courtyard. I suspect that many pieces of it were removed by looters after the house was abandoned; we did, however, find several round stone cylinders of the type the Aztecs called *chalchihuites*, circular emblems symbolizing water and its tutelary god Tlaloc.

We do not know who actually constructed the houses but at least some of the work must have involved specialists. Stone masonry, the laying of adobe bricks, roof preparation, plastering, and other tasks undoubtedly required special skills and there must have been enough continual construction at Tula to allow for full-time specialists. Building materials like tepetate and earth may have been free for the taking at the construction sites but adobe bricks, special clays, plaster, and timber probably had to be purchased. Large beams for roofs and doorjambs must have become scarce as time went on and may have been imported from distant upstream forests via the rivers.

Each house group had a small altar or shrine in the courtyard center. These took the form of rectangular or square platforms with sloping sides and horizontal tops. The outer surfaces were faced with a special veneer of small limestone fragments laid in horizontal rows and covered with plaster. We have named this veneer, which was frequently used on public and ceremonial buildings, Toltec Small Stone Construction.

plate 26

Since every courtyard altar we found had been more or less destroyed by looters at the time the houses were abandoned or shortly thereafter, we are uncertain about many of the construction details. However, we did find ten stone replicas of human skulls scattered around the exterior of the Central Group courtyard altar. They probably came from a frieze near the top of the structure. We also found a stone mask portraying a human face nearby, but its function is not known. Scattered human teeth in the altar fill suggest that it originally contained a burial which was removed by the looters, so the mask may have been part of an offering which they overlooked.

plate 27

The Central Group courtyard was surrounded by houses on raised platforms. The platform sides were covered with a Toltec Small Stone façade which had probably been plastered. Two stairways lead from the courtyard to the top of each house platform. In the case of House VI, one was a rather crude stone affair but the other was quite well made. Its steps consisted of well-dressed stones covered with plaster and it originally had balustrades at both ends. One of these was destroyed by looters in ancient times but the other still contained a carved stone tablet depicting two elaborately dressed men facing each other. The tablet was incorrectly placed with the figures vertical rather than horizontal because it fits the opening better that way, suggesting that it was a reused piece taken from an older building rather than something made specifically for this balustrade.

San Lorenzo, Monument 1. A typical Olmec colossal head possibly portraying a ruler.
Ht 2.8 m.

2 (*Above*) Round temple structure at Cuicuilco, Teotihuacan's early rival during the First Intermediate period.

3 (*Below*) Aerial photograph of Teotihuacan, the great pre-Columbian city which reached its zenith around AD 600. The Moon Pyramid is shown bottom left, the Sun Pyramid center left, and the rectangular Ciudadela at the far end of the main avenue (Street of the Dead).

4 (*Opposite*) Temple of Quetzalcoatl, Teotihuacan. The feathered serpent is Quetzalcoatl, the adjacent creature in the background, Tlaloc.

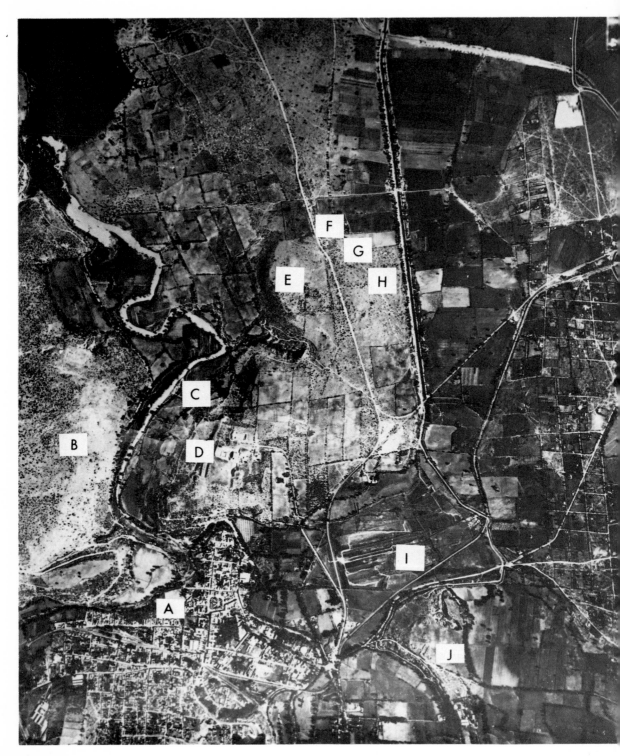

5 Aerial photograph of Tula and the surrounding region. A, Tula de Allende town; B, Cerro Mogone hill; C, Tula river; D, Tula Grande; E, Tula Chico; F, El Corral temple; G, Corral Locality excavation; H, Canal Locality excavation; I, El Salitre swamp; J, El Cielito hill.

6 Aerial photograph of Tula Grande. Left, Ballcourt I; center, Pyramid B and the Palacio Quemado; right, Pyramid C. The photograph was taken before the Atlantean statues were placed on the summit of Pyramid B.

7 Artist's reconstruction of Tula Grande. Left to right, Palacio Quemado, Pyramid B, Pyramid C. Foreground, Adoratorio. Note Jicuco mountain in the background (cf. plate I).

8 Tula Grande from the southwest, approximately the same vantage point as plate 7. Ballcourt II is in the foreground.

9 Pyramid C. The original façade was removed by Aztec looters and the restored walls are actually the mound interior.

10 Pyramid B from the south, with part of the Vestibule in the foreground.

11 The Palacio Quemado. The columns originally served as supports for the flat roofs of the colonnaded hall.

12 Ballcourt I, the western end. The large aprons on both sides defined the I-shaped playing field.

Tula relief carvings

3 (*Left above*) The east wall of Pyramid B. Jaguars and coyotes march across the upper bands; the lower registers show the god Tlahuizcalpantecuhtli and eagles eating human hearts.

4 (*Left below*) Detail of plate 13 showing Tlahuizcalpantecuhtli (Quetzalcoatl in the guise of Venus the Morning Star).

5 (*Right*) Detail of plate 13 showing an eagle eating a human heart.

6 (*Below*) Carved façade tablet from Pyramid B showing bundles of spears inserted in a human heart.

7 (*Left above*) The Coatepantli. This wall closed off the back or north side of Pyramid B.

8 (*Left below*) Relief carving on the Coatepantli. The repeated scene is that of a feathered rattlesnake devouring a partially skeletalized human figure, part of a Quetzalcoatl myth.

9 (*Above*) One of the polychrome benches in the Palacio Quemado showing a procession. The cornice is decorated with alternating Quetzalcoatls and Mixcoatls. For a detail, see plate IX.

10 (*Right*) Carved tablet from Tula depicting a standing jaguar. Precise provenance unknown. Ht 1.26 m.

Tula monumental sculpture

21 Atlantean roof supports for the temple on Pyramid B. The figures represent warriors carrying *atlatls* (spear throwers) in their hands. Ht 4.6 m.

22 Atlantean warrior roof support from Pyramid B. He wears the feathered helmet, butterfly pectoral, tied loin cloth, and sandals typical of Toltec warriors. Ht 4.6 m.

23 Small Atlantean warrior sculpture, carved from a single block of stone. From Tula but precise provenance unknown. Ht 1.15 m.

24 Broken Chac Mool found in the Palacio Quemado. The head has never been found. The only complete Chac Mool of the seven found at Tula is shown in plate XII.

Tula stone sculpture

25 (*Left*) Altar or bench support from Tula Grande in the form of a standing Atlantean figure. Exact provenance unknown.

26 (*Above*) Stone maskette. Possibly a death mask placed over the deceased persons face upon burial. Found adjacent to the Central Courtyard altar, Canal Locality.

The UMC excavations

27 (*Above*) Canal Locality. The Central Group courtyard and steps of House VI during excavation.

28 (*Center above*) Canal Locality. House walls constructed of roughly shaped pieces of limestone.

29 Corral Locality. Ceramic drainage tiles, originally inserted into a roof, as found *in situ*.

30 Canal Locality. Adobe block wall and lime plaster floor. (Length of ruler, 30 cm.)

31 (*Below right*) Canal Locality. Subfloor storage pit in House II. Nine foreign pottery vessels were found behind the furthest adobe block shelf support.

32 Corral Locality. Subfloor human burial in a typical Toltec interment position.

33 Corral Locality. Three-legged basalt metate as found *in situ*. (Cf. plate 52.)

34 UMC Project Laboratory, Tula de Allende. Students and workers process broken pottery after it has been washed.

The torrential summer rains forced Toltec builders to take special measures to prevent flooding of the houses. In some cases the ceramic tubes placed at roof edges emptied into open troughs which carried the water away from the buildings, and in two courtyards we came across drains at the low end. Although it is pure speculation, I believe that the rainwater was directed into as yet undiscovered reservoirs somewhere nearby for use during the winter dry season.

Many of the houses contained storage facilities of one sort or another. These varied in size and complexity from simple jars embedded in kitchen floors to large sunken pits in several rooms. The jars were so buried that only their necks or rims showed; they probably functioned as short-term storage of food or water used in preparing daily meals.

Two rooms in House II (Rooms 11 and 12) contained large square or rectangular pits which occupied a substantial area of the floor. The pit in the northwest corner of Room 11 was square and extended down to bedrock 1 m below the floor. The walls were lined with rectangular adobe blocks covered with a soft lime facing. The pit in Room 12 was constructed in a similar fashion but was rectangular and had a niche-like step at the northern end. *plate 31* Unlike its neighbor, it still contained some of its original contents. Three adobe blocks resting on the floor appear to have served as shelf supports, and at the back end of the pit behind the southern block we found nine imported pottery vessels in their original storage positions. The cache consisted of eight *plates 44, 46* goblets and one tripod bowl. Five of the goblets were Tohil Plumbate ware, a *plate XIV* lustrous pottery with a glaze-like finish which was manufactured on the Pacific coast of Chiapas and Guatemala. The remaining three goblets and the bowl were a Central American ware called Papagayo polychrome. The precise *plate XV* origin of the Papagayo vessels is not known but one Central American archaeologist has suggested they were made in eastern Honduras.

The presence of these rare and presumably valuable pots in the storage pit raises a number of questions. What were they used for? Do they indicate that the occupants of House II enjoyed higher status than the 'average' Toltec family? Why were they left behind when the house was abandoned? These questions I shall now attempt to answer.

The goblets probably functioned as drinking cups. Their nicked bases, scratches, and worn rim paint suggest they had seen much use before they were put away for the last time. Given their apparent value and the fact that they were stored in a special place, it seems likely that they were only brought out on special occasions such as rituals and feasts. I can well imagine their owners using them to serve guests frothy bitter chocolate or the fine pulque for which the Tula area is still famous today.

Although Plumbate ware is the most common foreign trade pottery at Tula, it is rare enough to suggest that it was an expensive prestige possession. The Papagayo pots are the only ones known from anywhere in central Mexico and certainly indicate the high status or unusual buying power of those who possessed them. Most Toltecs probably could not afford one such vessel brought from so far away, let alone an entire drinking service.

Why were such valuable possessions left behind when the house was abandoned? Perhaps the occupants left in such a hurry that they did not have time to retrieve them, although we did not find any evidence to support this hypothesis. I am inclined to believe that, being hidden behind the adobe block at the far end of the pit, they were simply overlooked.

In addition to the jars and pits, we suspect that certain entire rooms were devoted to storage. Many of these rooms were created by partitioning existing rooms after the buildings had been in use for a while, most being so small that it is difficult to envisage any other use than for storage. Unfortunately whatever they contained was either removed or was perishable, because we did not find anything to suggest their original contents.

plate 32

Toltec houses sheltered the dead as well as the living; the deceased were normally buried in or near the house rather than in special cemeteries. The most common practice was to place the body in a pit under the house floor. At times offerings of a few pots were placed with the dead, perhaps for use in the afterlife. In some cases the interments lacked non-perishable grave goods of any sort. Every courtyard altar probably contained a burial but these structures had been looted to such an extent that it is difficult to be certain. I suspect that the altar burials were those of high status individuals, perhaps the top ranking elders of kin groups, whose memory was kept alive through rituals at the altars. We found only six definite burials in our excavations but might have found many more if we had spent more time digging below house floors. Alternatively, it is possible that certain individuals were cremated, as the historical sources indicate, though there were no signs of their ashes. As will be seen in the discussion of the Corral Locality, not everybody was given a formal burial; sacrificial victims whose bodies were cannibalized were simply tossed on to rubbish dumps in abandoned rooms.

A final architectural feature of interest in the Canal Locality was a kiln for firing ceramic objects in an open patio in House VIII. It consisted of two parallel rock and clay chambers built into the floor when the house was constructed. The above-floor sections were all but destroyed, whilst the *in situ* remnants were severely burned. Dan Healan's study of the kiln shows that a sophisticated duct system forced air through the furnace chamber into the firing chamber which held the objects being baked. In order to retain the heat while the kiln was in use, the open top was covered with large potsherds and stones. We were baffled by the structure when it was being excavated, but some of the local workers who are also potters immediately identified it as a kiln and explained that they too cover their kilns with large potsherds. A pile of debris including potsherd covers and six ceramic drainage tubes lay alongside the kiln. The drainage tubes were probably fired in it, for the firing chamber is of an unusual shape and seems to have been designed to accommodate them nicely.

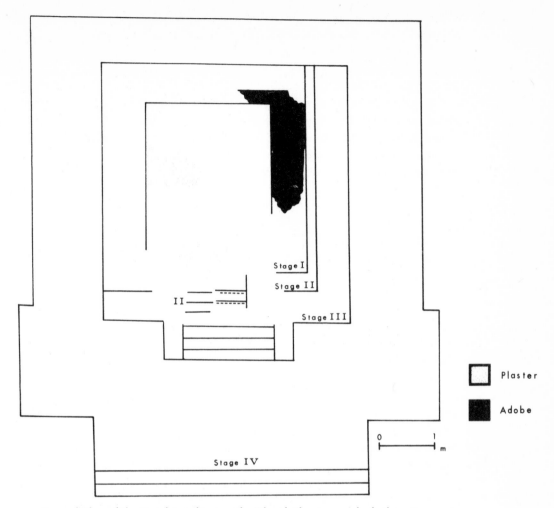

21 *Ground plan of the Canal Locality temple. The platform was rebuilt three times (Stages II–IV) after its initial construction. The adobe is in situ wall debris from the shrine, the plaster is part of the shrine floor.*

The East Group temple

The East Group consists of a small temple surrounded by rooms and patios. The temple was a rubble-filled platform faced with a Toltec Small Stone Construction façade which supported a tiny two-room shrine. Stocker detected four construction stages in the platform, all of which took place during the Tollan phase. The Stage I platform measured 4.5 × 3.8 m and was 1.0 m high. A stairway on the west side led from the clay patio to the shrine. The shrine had a porch-like antechamber and an enclosed interior room. The platform was enlarged slightly during Stage II and the original stairway covered by a new one, though the shrine was left intact. Stage III involved

fig. 21

91

minor modifications to the platform, construction of a new balustraded stairway, and enlargement of the shrine. Substantial changes took place during Stage IV. The platform was enlarged to 7.2 × 8.5 m, small wing-like appendages were added to the north and south sides, and a much wider stairway without balustrades was constructed. The shrine was also enlarged.

The artifacts found around the temple indicate that it was devoted to the Tlaloc cult. Brazier fragments with the rain god's face modeled on their sides were scattered around the periphery of the structure and carved stone *chalchihuites* were found in positions suggesting they had formed a band around the upper walls of the shrine. The area behind the stairs, a favorite spot for dedicatory caches, had been looted in ancient times. Nevertheless we did find an unusual figurine, missed by the looters, which portrays an individual holding two smaller people or babies at his waist, a theme sometimes associated with Tlaloc. Three Pacific coast shells and a turtle carapace found around the temple can also be associated with water and Tlaloc; the carapace may be the remains of a ceremonial drum.

Why do we find a rain god temple in a residential zone occupied by people who probably were not farmers? Actually this is part of a much larger question which has bothered us for years; namely, who lived in the Canal Locality and what place did they occupy in Toltec society? At times I suspect the entire area was inhabitied by priests or religious specialists. The previously mentioned straight lines and other indications of a Tula city grid found by Mastache and Crespo seem to form large 'neighborhoods', or *barrios*, approximately 600 m on a side with a concentration of large structures which are probably temples in one corner. The Canal Locality appears to lie in one of these corners and a large temple mound is located a few meters west of our excavations. If the Canal Locality residents were the spiritual and political leaders of the *barrio*, the large number of storage facilities make sense because the residents needed them for storing costumes, ritual paraphernalia, and the 'gifts' or taxes they received from their followers. The large temple mound may have been their main theater of public operations and the East Group temple a personal shrine for worship of their own tutelary god. All of this is speculation and we hope to clarify some of the interpretations as we finish the analyses, but only renewed excavations can really resolve the issues.

The Corral Locality

Margaret Mandeville's excavation 50 m southeast of the Corral temple exposed a small section of an elaborate Tollan phase structure. Unfortunately the depth of the debris and complicated architecture prevented us from uncovering a wider area in the time available to us. This is regrettable, because the building was quite different from the houses at the Canal Locality and may in fact have been a special structure associated with the Ehecatl temple, rather than an ordinary house.

fig. 22

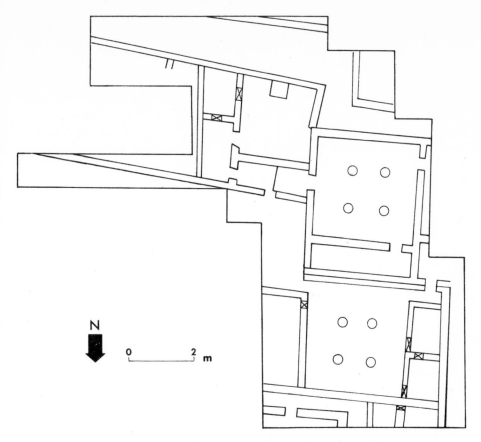

22 Ground plan of the Corral Locality. Circles indicate column bases, X's represent doorways blocked up late in the building's history.

The excavated section of the structure was a rectangular block of rooms. There is no evidence that they were constructed around an open courtyard, but too small an area had been exposed for this possibility to be ruled out. The fill soil brought in to raise the ground level prior to construction contained Corral and Terminal Corral phase pottery but the rooms were all constructed and abandoned during the Tollan phase.

Stone was the preferred construction material. Wall foundations were built of rough field stones laid in mud mortar, and dressed stones were used for most of the above-ground walls. Adobe blocks were employed for interior partition walls in some cases. Many of the walls had apparently been covered with lime plaster or fine mud facings. Doorways were framed with well-cut rectangular stone blocks and one had a stone basal socket with a well-worn hole suggestive of a pivoting door. Almost half of the doorways were subsequently sealed off, but we do not known if this was all done at one time or not. Only one lime plaster floor was encountered, the others were constructed of packed earth.

The building possessed several unusual architectural features. It had ceramic tile roof drains like those in the Canal Locality but we also discovered two unusual U-shaped stone troughs which apparently formed part of the drain system. Although Acosta found similar drains on the side of the Palacio de Quetzalcoatl east of Pyramid B, ours were the first to be encountered outside Tula Grande.

Room 6 contained a rectangular altar placed against the south wall. The outer walls had what Mesoamericanists call a *talud* and *tablero* configuration; the talud is an inward-sloping base and the tablero consisted of an inset panel surrounded by a border of dressed stones. The altar sides were finished with a Toltec Small Stone Construction façade constructed of broken potsherds laid horizontally rather than the usual limestone fragments, and the top was made of flat stones placed in earth mortar. A burial chamber beneath the altar contained a seated male adult skeleton whose skull was missing. The presence of a few upper teeth in the surrounding soil suggests that the skull was removed after the burial had been in place a while, perhaps to be reused as a sacred relic of some sort. The body had been buried in a tightly flexed posture and was accompanied by an offering of three pots. A small pit constructed of metate fragments and flat rocks was found 20 cm north of the altar, but its purpose is not clear because it was empty.

Rooms 1 and 3 contained stone bases for roof columns. The absence of debris from the columns suggests they were made of wood beams. The bases formed two sets of four each and appear to have been added after the rooms were in use for a while. They were constructed by digging circular holes down through the floors to bedrock. The holes were filled with field stones and earth mortar and capped with flat stones at the floor level. Three bases in Room 3 contained thousands of tiny fossilized starfish which appear to have been deposited in a leather pouch or some other perishable container. One cache also included a quartz crystal and another had a Pacific coast Olivella shell. The positions of the column bases suggest that the rooms had skylights similar to those in the Palacio Quemado and other Tula Grande buildings.

The functions of the Corral Locality rooms are not easy to interpret, and the situation is aggravated by the fact that some of them were renovated at least once during the building's history. Room 3 may have functioned as a kitchen, for the floor contained a mano, metate, hearth, and discarded animal bones. Room 9 apparently served as a hallway or corridor. We suspect that Room 6 was a shrine chamber because of the altar in it and the seclusion implied in the roundabout access through Rooms 5 and 7. Several of the smaller rooms (4, 8, and 14) were sealed off at some point by blocking up the doorways.

The frequent occurrence of fragmentary human skeletons and miscellaneous human bones mixed with other debris on and above the room floors is one of the most puzzling features of the Corral Locality. Room 3 contained so many human remains that we dubbed it 'the bone room', but similar finds were made in Room 9 and elsewhere. These were not burials, nor do they seem to be the unburied remains of victims of some final tragedy when the building was abandoned. The best explanation we can offer is that this occurred while the Corral temple was still in use, the building being converted into a dump for temple refuse, including the remains of sacrificial victims. The casual and disrespectful treatment of the bodies suggests this manner of death, and there is more than a mere hint that they were then cannibalized.

What was the nature of the Corral Locality structure and what its purpose? We did not expose enought to provide a satisfactory answer to these questions, but we suspect it was not an ordinary residence. Its proximity to the Corral temple, unusual ground plan, and elaborate architecture all suggest a special function, perhaps as a domicile for priests or a priestly school of the type the Aztecs called *calmecacs*. Changes in the use to which it was put in the course of time are indicated by the renovations, and the rooms ultimately became rubbish dumps after their original functions ceased. Mandeville and I have always regretted that we did not expose more of this mysterious building.

How well did Toltec houses provide for the basic needs of the inhabitants? The answer to this question depends in part on one's culturally conditioned expectations, but they seem to have been adequate from many aspects.

In the first place, they were well adapted to the climate and general physical environment. In addition to being made from locally abundant materials, they were comfortable. The thick adobe walls absorbed heat slowly and kept the house interior cool during the day. At night they retained the absorbed heat and protected the inhabitants from the surprisingly low and at times bitter night temperatures. Furthermore heat from a small fire was held in the room and not dissipated, as happens with wood or wattle and daub structures. The adobe walls not only contributed to the comfort of the inhabitants but were durable and lasted for generations. The stone wall foundations and basal mounds insured dry floors and avoided the problem of adobe deterioration due to absorbed moisture from the ground, and the hazard of flooding was minimized by the flat roofs and drainage sytems.

Houses must cater for the social as well as the physical needs of the occupants. The arrangement of Toltec houses around central courtyards facilitated close intercourse among the residents. The occupants probably were kinsmen who formed a social microcosm within the larger urban society: a wieldy group of predictable personalities with clear lines of authority and responsibility. The large, impersonal, and partially unknown – hence unpredictable – outside world could be shut out by staying inside one house group, and the desire for privacy is evident in every aspect of the architecture.

The arrangement of functional spaces within house groups provided comfortable communal working quarters in the courtyard and allowed each family its own privacy when it was desired. In addition, the architectural units were easily modified to meet changing requirements. Rooms could be enlarged or divided as families grew or declined, and their functions changed as needs dictated.

Finally, the houses provided links to the supernatural world through the altars and other ritual facilities. The individual could worship the most important deities in a personal or familial setting, rather than as a member of a crowd straining to catch a glimpse of distant priests at the summit of a temple. All in all, then, the houses filled the physical, social and spiritual needs of their occupants. What more could a Toltec or even a twentieth-century university professor ask of a home?

7 The Toltec economy

There are two reasons why we made the Toltec economy a primary concern of the UMC Project. First, archaeologists can study economics more easily than many other aspects of life, because virtually everything they find reflects the economy in one way or another. The second reason is that I am a moderately strong believer in a theory and research strategy which anthropologists call cultural materialism. This theory maintains that economics constitutes at least one of, if not *the*, crucial factor in the history and evolution of human culture and civilization. The research strategy involves studying the economic structures and relationships within a society and attempting to understand how they worked, their effects on the rest of the culture, and why they had these effects. Although much remains to be learned about the economy of the Toltecs and its impact on their history, we have made a substantial beginning toward this goal. Our information deals with three major sectors or components of the Toltec economy; agriculture, craft production, and commerce. In each case we know something about the products, production techniques and organization, and exchange arrangements.

Agriculture

Virtually all we know about the Toltecs is based on information from the city of Tula, but we must remember that they were an agrarian society predominantly composed of peasant farmers living in small villages and hamlets outside the city. These peasants grew the foods and fibers which permitted the elaboration of the urban economy and even the basic existence of the city. Unfortunately almost nothing is known about life in these rural communities because none of the sites has been excavated.

Sahagun's informants praised Toltec farmers so lavishly that their comments read like a modern Chamber of Commerce brochure. The following statement is typical: 'It is said all the squashes were very large, and some were quite round. And the ears of corn were as large as hand grinding stones (manos) and long, they could hardly be carried in one's arms. And the amaranth plants – verily, they climbed up them; they could be climbed. And also colored cotton prospered – bright red, yellow, rose colored, violet, green, azure, verdigris color, whitish, brown, shadowy, rose red, and coyote colored. All different colored cottons were this way; so they grew, they did not dye them.'[1] These accounts must be viewed skeptically; even though native American cotton grew naturally in various hues, there is no evidence for its cultivation in the cold arid Tula area and the maize cobs and amaranth bushes described would have been the talk of the annual Missouri State Fair.

Maize was the basic Toltec staple and the numerous maize fragments, grinding stones, and *comal* (tortilla griddle) sherds in our collections indicate its central place in the daily lives of the people. We do not know how many varieties were grown or what yields farmers received for their efforts. The short growing season and scant moisture must have favored small-eared plants which matured rapidly. These assured the farmers of at least some harvest but produced less grain than other types grown in more favorable parts of central Mexico. Larger, more productive varieties which took longer to mature may have been sown in choice irrigated fields where they could get a head start before the beginning of the rainy season.

Tortillas and other maize foods were supplemented with secondary foods which added variety to the diet and helped to balance it. Beans (*Phaseolus sp.*) were second to maize, although they have not yet been identified in archaeological deposits. We found remains of chili peppers (*Capsicum sp.*), amaranth seeds (*Amaranthus sp.*), squashes (*Cucurbita sp.*) and maguey (*Agave sp.*), all of which are also mentioned in the written sources. Chili sauces were served as condiments and added many minor but essential nutritional elements to the diet. Amaranth seeds were ground into a paste from which small cakes were made, and squashes were consumed as a cooked vegetable. Magueys provided two foods: the hearts were roasted and the sap was fermented into a mildly alcoholic beverage called *pulque*. In addition maguey plants provided thorns for needles and ceremonial bloodletters, and the dried leaves were used for fuel in an area where wood was scarce.

Nutritious wild seeds and seasonal fruits relieved some of the monotony of the diet and provided emergency foods in lean times prior to the fall harvest. The preserved plant remains we found included mesquite (*Prosopis sp.*), chenopodium (*Chenopodium sp.*), the cherry-like capulin (*Prunus sp.*), persimmon (*Diospyrus sp.*), and the ubiquitous prickly pear (*Opuntia sp.*).

Meat was a rare festival food where most people were concerned. Turkeys and small dogs were the only meat-producing domestic animals and both were identified by Bob Gilbert in the excavated faunal remains. Domesticated bees provided honey, which was highly prized in the absence of other sweets. While most of the wild animals in the area were considered suitable for the stewpot, our samples produced only deer, jackrabbit, and cottontail rabbit with any frequency. The burnt human bones found in our excavations indicate that human flesh was considered edible. The bones probably came from sacrificial victims who were slaves. The frequency of cannibalism is not known; much has been written recently about the possible importance of it among the Aztecs, but the situation at Tula can only be clarified by additional research. Sahagun's sources insisted that human sacrifice, and presumably the associated cannibalism, were absent at Tula until after Quetzalcoatl's defeat and flight, but this seems very unlikely.

Toltec farming practices and techniques must have been similar to those reported for their contact-period descendents. Two major types of fields were cultivated; large *milpas* located outside the villages and small gardens adjacent to the houses. The *milpas* contained the major maize, bean, and squash crops; the garden crops included some maize and a host of minor items.

Winter frosts and a single rainy season meant that all farming was done during the spring and summer. The land was cleared with stone axes and the rubbish burned so that the ash fertilized the soil. The earth was probably worked with stone or wooden hoes and planted with wooden digging sticks called *coas*. Beans were placed in open spaces between the maize, and cucurbits such as squash were allowed to grow among the maize plants. Fields were weeded several times during the growing season and mounds of soil were put around the base of the maturing maize plants to prevent wind damage. At harvest time the maize stalks were bent over to allow the grain to harden on the cob while keeping out birds and moisture. Harvested ears were stored in the house, and grain was removed from the cobs with bone or antler-tine huskers as it was needed.

Irrigation was absolutely essential for successful agriculture in the Toltec heartland and, as mentioned earlier, Tula is situated in the largest zone of irrigable land in this rather marginal part of central Mexico. Mexican archaeologists have discovered many as yet undated ancient canals and other irrigation features around Tula, which must have functioned during Toltec times.[2] Canals were simple ditches which received water from rivers, springs, and temporary streams. Brush and earth dams directed the water into feeder canals and on to the fields. Irrigation and summer rains provided enough water for successful harvests, but dependence on rainfall alone meant frequent crop failure. Since irrigation water ultimately depends on rainfall, Tlaloc and his subordinates in the pantheon of water deities were critically important to every Toltec.

In addition to irrigation the Toltecs apparently constructed hillside terraces. The Tula region contains numerous undated remains of pre-Columbian stone-walled terraces built to trap water and silt. Similar modern systems in central Mexico are highly productive but require hard work to build and maintain. Modern farmers use them only when they do not have access to other lands; as when population growth outstrips the available land resources or large landholders monopolize the lion's share of good farmland. The same was probably true in ancient times and I suspect the terraces were built as a response to population pressure near the end of the Tollan phase.

The small house gardens were more intensively cultivated than the *milpas*. The extra care included fertilization with ashes, green manure, and human waste matter; hand irrigation, using pots; and careful weeding. In addition to basic foodstuffs they probably contained condiments, herbs, medicinal plants, fruit trees, and magueys. They might have provided up to 25 to 30 percent of a family's food supply and were an essential buffer against starvation in bad years.

Toltec peasants had to grow more than just what they themselves ate. They had to harvest a 'surplus' in order to purchase tools, clothing, household utensils, foods they did not themselves grow, and the services of specialists such as healers and priests. In addition, nobody escaped the tax collectors, who made certain the state received its share. The taxes supported rulers, priests, soldiers and others who provided protection and services for the peasants; and even if these services seemed unduly expensive, they had no choice but to participate in the system. In reality, Toltec peasant households were the basic elements in complex economic and social webs rather than isolated self-sufficient entities.

Craft production

Besides signifying 'inhabitant of Tula', the term Toltec meant 'master craftsman' or 'artisan'. Sixteenth-century writers paid great tribute to the skills of Toltec artisans. Returning once more to Sahagun, we read that 'many of them [the Toltecs] were scribes, lapidarians, carpenters, stone cutters, masons, feather workers, feather gluers, potters, spinners, weavers. They were very learned. They discovered, they knew of green stones, fine turquoise, common turquoise, the turquoise land. They went to learn of, to seek out, the mines of silver, gold, copper, tin, mica, lead. They went to learn of all of them. They went to seek out all the mines of amber, or rock crystal, of amethyst; they went to marvel at the pearls, the opals. All which now exists is their discovery – the necklaces, the arm bands. Of that which is precious, however, some is forgotten, some lost.'[3] Of feather-working, among Mesoamerica's most exalted art forms, we read, 'The Tolteca were skilled, it is said they were the feather workers who glued feathers. In ancient times they took charge of gluing feathers; and it was really their discovery, for in ancient times they used the shields, the devices, those called *apanecaoitl*, which were their exclusive property. When the wonderful devices were entrusted to them, they prepared, they glued the feathers, they indeed formed works of art, they performed works of skill. In truth they invented all the wonderful, precious, marvelous things which they made.'[4]

If we accept these glowing accounts, the Toltecs were the master craftsmen of Mesoamerica. However, as mentioned previously, many of their predecessors and even their Aztec descendents surpassed them in craftsmanship and artistic abilities. Thus it appears that these descriptions either reflect different standards of beauty or an attempt to glorify the informants' putative ancestors. We must also remember that many of the things mentioned have not survived Aztec looting and the passage of time, or else remain to be discovered. For example, Toltec art shows men wearing elaborate jewelry

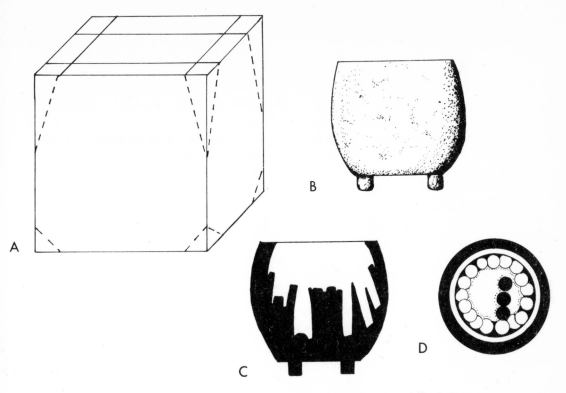

23 Basic steps in the manufacture tecali vessels. A, stringsawing the original block; B, final exterior shape; C, core removal by levels; D, step C as seen from above (black core holes are on the second or lower level).

plate 51

which has never been found by archaeologists. Future discoveries of intact upper class tombs or the excavation of élite craft workshops may yet justify the claims of Sahagun's informants.

In Aztec society the élite crafts were practiced by artisans belonging to hereditary guilds. The guild members frequently formed distinct ethnic and linguistic enclaves in Aztec cities and at least some had been invited or persuaded to settle there by their noble patrons. The same was undoubtedly true at Tula, and I am confident that someday we will find evidence of them in the archaeological remains.

We only have direct archaeological evidence for one élite craft at Tula, the working of *tecali*. *Tecali* or travertine is a white sedimentary stone, often confused with onyx, which Mesoamericans used for beads, ornaments, bowls, jars, and other luxury products.

An unfinished globular jar found on the surface at Tula several years ago allowed Mexican archaeologist Noemi Castillo Tejera to reconstruct the following steps in the manufacturing process.[5] First a rectangular block of raw material was quarried, perhaps in a source area near Tula. Then the exterior

fig. 23

shape was roughed out by sawing off chunks of waste material with cords and abrasive, and the exterior was smoothed by patient sanding with a wet abrasive. After the exterior was finished, the interior was hollowed out by removing cylindrical cores of matrix material with hollow reed or birdbone drills. (The jar Tejera described was lost or thrown away when less than half the interior had been removed.) The final steps were to smooth and polish the vessel inside and out, then perhaps paint the exterior.

We found nineteen cylindrical *tecali* cores at various places in our excavations. At first we thought perhaps our houses had been occupied by *tecali* craftsmen but the evidence does not bear this out. We did not find any other manufacturing debris and since a single vessel would produce sixty or seventy cores, a workshop should contain thousands of them.[6] In all likelihood our house occupants obtained the cores from *tecali* craftsmen in order to use them for some purpose unknown to us.

Although Tula's élite crafts were its claim to fame, the production of common utilitarian objects was the key to its economic success and the major source of employment for many urban families. Production of pottery, figurines, stone tools, building stone, adobe blocks, baskets, mats, cloth, wooden implements, and other mundane items gave employment to thousands of people, as opposed to the hundreds who practiced élite crafts. Although we know virtually nothing about most of these crafts, we do have some insights into the ceramics and stone tool industries.

Every Toltec family used pottery vessels daily and the Tula ceramics industry supplied a potential market of at least 20,000 families or 100,000 people in the city and its hinterland. Every kitchen needed storage jars, food preparation utensils, serving dishes, and eating vessels; also many households used braziers, incense burners, and other non-culinary vessels. Storage jars for grain and water were round or globular and frequently had necks. Whilst many had plain exteriors, decorations such as horizontal red bands, polished red surfaces, and crosshatched white-painted designs resembling a woven mat were common.

Cooking and food-preparation vessels included large bowls, *comals*, and *fig. 24* *molcajetes*, small or medium-sized hemispherical bowls with tripod supports. Bowls were used for stews and other liquid foods; they had flat bottoms, flared walls, and loop handles on the rim for hanging over the fire. Tollan phase *comals* or tortilla griddles were brown circular plates with raised rims and roughened bottoms which helped conduct the heat evenly. Crosshatched incisions on the interior were used for grinding chili peppers and other sauce ingredients. Some had crudely painted designs over the brown base color and molded supports in the form of a serpent and other animal heads.

Serving and eating vessels included flat dishes and hemispherical bowls *plates 37, 38* similar to *molcajetes* but lacking incisions on the interior. Orange wares with occasional incised designs and buff-brown wares sometimes decorated with red-painted motifs were the most common types. Three supports in the shape

24 *Toltec domestic or utilitarian pottery. From top to bottom: rows 1–4, 6, and 8 are bowls, row 5 is a comal, row 7 are jars.*

of small solid clay nubs, or larger hollow feet with clay pellet rattles were quite popular. Complex decorations on some plates and bowls indicate that they served as an important medium of artistic expression for both the potters and the users. The fact that most decorations had a cult significance is just one indication of the religious sense that permeated Toltec life.

Cylindrical or hourglass-shaped ceramic braziers were often used as stoves and many show the effects of intense burning on the interior. Their rims frequently have finger-impressed clay strips; the more elaborate examples feature appliquéd buttons, spikes, or Tlaloc faces. Whereas the simpler ones were used in houses, it seems the fancier vessels held ceremonial fires in temples.

plates 39, 40

Two types of censers were used for burning copal resin during rituals. 'Frying pan' censers having bowls with flared walls and tubular handles are usually found in temple contexts. Openwork censers had small globular pots with handles. The pots have carved latticework openings in the bodies, red-painted rims, two small supports, and skulls and other religious motifs on their surfaces. Since they are found in both temple and household debris, they may have had a different function from that of the 'frying pan' censer.

fig. 25

Mastache and Crespo have tentatively identified surface remains of ceramic workshops in the city, though none have been excavated. The surface indications suggest that some workshops specialized in making specific pottery types. The standardized vessel forms and decorations suggest fulltime artisans who devoted their lives to the trade. Most of the pots were formed by hand rather than in molds, and often the firing was so poorly controlled that it must have been done in open-ground hearths rather than special kilns like that found in House VIII.

Despite the lack of archaeological excavation in workshops, we were able to learn a great deal about the Toltec pottery industry by observing modern potters in the area. Some of our excavation workers are potters who use essentially pre-Columbian techniques to produce imitation Toltec pottery for sale to tourists. Margaret Mandeville investigated them in 1971 and collected information of great archaeological interest.

The potters obtain clays from two different sources at the banks of the Rio Tula.[7] The basic raw material formed by mixing the clays does not require a special additive, or temper, which potters frequently use to prevent cracking during the drying and firing stages. The vessels are formed by molding and hand modelling, and then allowed to dry in the air for 24 hours. Next, the surfaces are scraped and carefully polished. Decorations are added by incising or painting designs and the pots are polished once more. After three or four days the completely dried vessels are fired in a crude kiln or in an open fire built directly on the ground.

plate 47

Mandeville noted the amount of time her informants spent making and decorating different kinds of imitation Toltec pots. Since the value of any manufactured object depends in part on how much time is spent on it, we

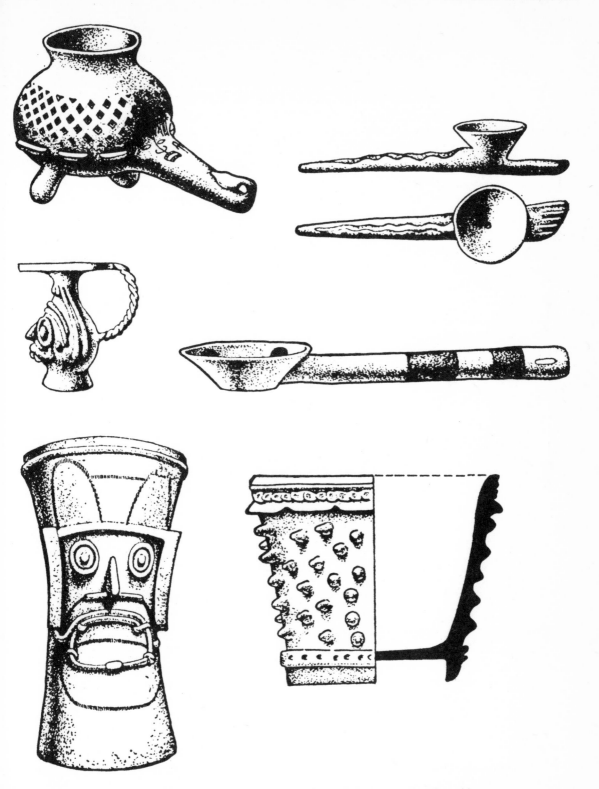

25 Toltec ritual pottery. Top left, open-work handled censer; top right, tobacco pipe; middle left, Tlaloc effigy jar; middle right, frying-pan censer; lower left, Tlaloc effigy brazier; lower right, spiked brazier.

assumed that we could roughly calculate the relative values of different kinds of pottery in ancient Tula based on this measure. We also tried to estimate how many vessels one person could produce in a year and how many potters were needed to supply Tula and the surrounding area.

As might be expected, elaborate painting or incision increased the time spent on a vessel but not as much as one might expect. An undecorated plate took 40 minutes to produce while elaborate decoration added 30 minutes to the manufacturing time. The corresponding figures for small jars were 60 and 80 minutes, and for small bowls 65 and 110 minutes respectively. These figures suggest that elaborate vessels were more valuable than plain ones, at least in terms of the time spent manufacturing them. However, we must remember that factors other than manufacturing time enter into the value of a pot. These factors might include the skill of the potter, the desirability of unusual shapes or motifs, and the deliberate lowering of production rates to keep the price of each piece artificially high.

Mandeville estimated that a fulltime potter could produce 675–2,500 small vessels annually, depending on the type of vessel and amount of decoration. Modern ethnographic studies in other parts of rural Mexico show that peasant kitchens normally contain about 60 vessels and that the average life expectancy of a pot is about six months, depending on how it is used.

These figures, which are based on small vessels which can be made rapidly, can be used to make several interesting if speculative calculations about Tula's ceramics industry. If the city contained 7,500 households (35,000 people divided by an average family size of five persons), 450,000 pottery vessels were in use at any one time and 900,000 pots were consumed annually. The INAH surveys suggest that Tula's hinterland contained at least 60,000 inhabitants.[8] If all their pottery was produced at Tula, they consumed an additional 1,440,000 vessels annually. Thus the urban potters had to produce at least 2,340,000 pots each year. If a Toltec potter produced an average of 1,000 vessels annually, 2,340 potters were needed to fulfil the demand. Assuming that each potter was a family head, 2,340 of Tula's 7,500 households, or almost one-third of the urban population, were involved in the ceramics industry. These figures are very crude approximations and many unknown factors would affect them, but they do suggest the important role this industry played in the Toltec economy.

Figurines were another common Toltec ceramic product. They were
figs 26–28 manufactured by pressing wet clay into clay molds, removing them for air drying, firing, and painting. The backs of many figurine still retain fingerprints the artisans neglected to wipe away. The use of molds is a puzzling feature. At first glance it appears to be a mass-production technique allowing rapid manufacture of many identical items; however, virtually every figurine in the collection studied by Terrance Stocker was unique and required a different mold, hardly a time-saving procedure. Figurine workshops have not been positively identified at Tula but concentrations of figurines and molds at two places in the city suggest potential workshop locations. Humans are the most

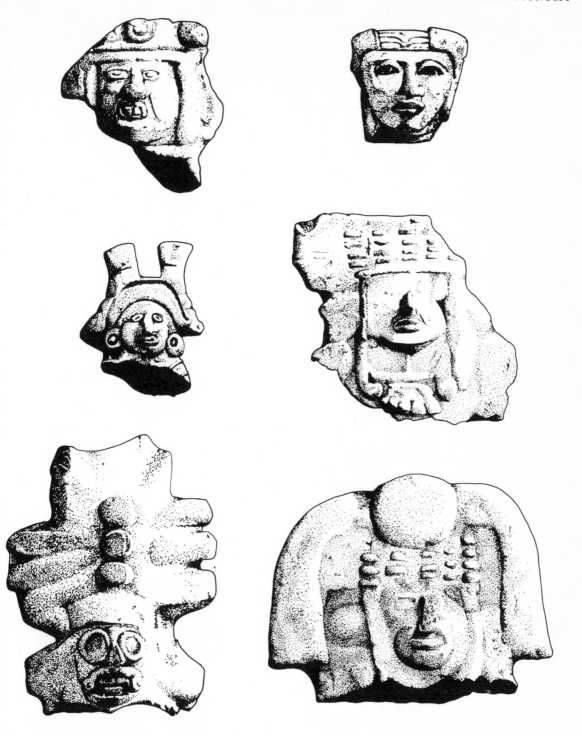

26 Figurine heads. Bottom left, Tlaloc; center and bottom right, moldmade 'gingerbread' pieces. Top right, Teotihuacan style; center left, Aztec; remainder, Tollan phase.

27 Tollan phase flat 'gingerbread'-type figurine. The sketchy details were supplemented with multi-colored painted designs. Ht 12 cm.

28 (below) Tollan phase figurine bodies. Top row, flat, moldmade 'gingerbread' types, possibly females, based on the skirt-like garments. Bottom row, Toltec warriors wearing loincloths, chest ornaments, and quilted cotton armor. Below left, Ht 4 cm.

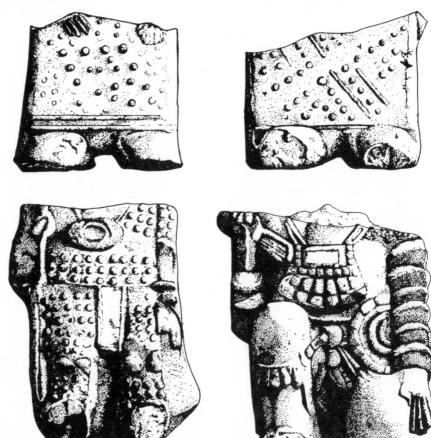

29 *A wheeled animal effigy figurine from Panuco, Veracruz. Fragments of numerous such objects were found in the UMC Project excavations.*

common subjects portrayed on Tollan phase figurines. Flat 'gingerbread' figurines depicting women with elaborate coiffures, stylized faces and long skirts are the most distinctive type. Many still retain traces of complex designs painted after firing. Among the colors are blue, white, black, and yellow. Most of the paint has disappeared but enough remains to show that the combinations varied considerably, perhaps depending on the specific purpose the figurine user had in mind. Male figurines emphasized warriors wearing masks, helmets, quilted cotton armour, and shields. Only a few deities are portrayed, notably Tlaloc and the goddess Xochiquetzal.

plates 48–50

Figurines of animals include birds, felines, dogs and other canids. Some have holes in the legs for axles to which wheels were attached. The common belief that American Indians were ignorant of the wheel is not strictly true, as these and similar figurines at other Second Intermediate Period sites indicate. But because wheeled vehicles were useless without large draft animals, its practical applications were never developed, and it was the Toltecs' misfortune that horses and camels were eliminated from their environment by their ancestors during Archaic times.

fig. 29

The functions of figurines are not clear. They seem to be much more common in household debris than around temples and other public buildings.

Most are broken, many in ways suggesting the user deliberately snapped them into two pieces while holding them in his hands. My guess is that they were used to rid sick people of malignant spirits during healing rituals, and were broken to insure destruction of the cause of the illness.

plate 33 The production of ground stone tools, particularly manos and metates, was another basic Toltec craft. Most Tollan phase metates were rectangular concave slabs of vesicular basalt with two small legs on the back, or low, end and a taller one in front. Manos were oblong handstones resembling modern rolling pins which were pushed back and forth across the metate while grinding maize. Microscopic stone fragments from manos and metates got incorporated into the maize flour and frequently produced a characteristic type of wear or polish on the teeth of Toltec skeletons.[9]

The manufacture of manos and metates involved quarrying the stone, pecking out the approximate shape with stone tools, and grinding the blank into its final form with wet sand or some other abrasive. Every kitchen needed plate 52 at least one mano-metate set, but as they lasted for years a woman consumed relatively few in her lifetime. The number of people employed in making them is impossible to calculate but it must have been only a fraction of those involved in ceramics and obsidian tool manufacture.

Other ground stone objects such as beads, mortars, pestles, axes, and celts are found in small quantities. Mortars are rare, probably because ceramic *molcajetes* served the same function and were less expensive. Axes and celts occur infrequently in urban houses because the inhabitants had little need for them, though a sizeable market may have existed in the rural villages.

Tools made of obsidian were another basic necessity for the average Toltec household and the demand for them fostered a major industry in the city. This volcanic glass is found in scattered deposits in the Mesoamerican highlands and has several advantages over other substances as a raw material for cutting tools. It will keep a sharp edge almost equal to that of a steel blade, can be worked with various knapping techniques, and occurs in large accessible deposits on or near the earth's surface.

The quantity of obsidian debris found at Tula is remarkable. The Urban Zone Survey collected more than 15,000 pieces from less than one percent of the site surface and at least 25,000 pieces were found in the excavations. Double-edged prismatic blades were most prevalent but knives, scrapers, projectile points, and small ornaments were manufactured as well.

Alice Benfer, Dan Healan, Terrance Stocker, and Robert Cobean have studied various aspects of the Toltec obsidian industry. Although their studies are still in progress, we already know the sources of the raw materials, the basic manufacturing steps, and something about the distribution of the final products.

Recent advances in nuclear physics and trace element analyses enable scientists to determine the source of any piece of obsidian. All types of obsidian contain the same basic chemicals but materials from different sources have different quantities of minor or trace elements such as manganese, zinc, and rubidium. Thus comparison of the trace element composition of a tool with that of known deposits enables us to pinpoint the origin of the raw material. Preliminary results of such studies suggest that 90 percent of the Tula obsidian came from Pachuca, Hidalgo and Zinapecuaro, Michoacan.[10]

The Pachuca source is a large group of outcrops in the mountains east of the Hidalgo state capital. The shimmering green-gold obsidian found there was esteemed for its beauty and traded throughout Mesoamerica in ancient times. Every central Mexican civilization tried to control either the source itself or the distribution of its products. It is almost certain that the mines and their products were under direct Toltec control, because at least 80 percent of the Tula obsidian studied so far came from there.

plate 53

The Zinapecuaro source lies about 63 miles west of Tula. The grey obsidian found there was not widely used in ancient times and the fact that it accounts for perhaps 10 percent of Tula's obsidian is surprising. We do not know whether the Toltecs controlled Zinapecuaro; In my view they did not, but received their supply from there as tribute or by way of trade.

Obsidian tools were manufactured in four basic steps. The raw material was quarried; excess waste was removed at the quarry; partially reduced blocks called 'preforms' were carried to the urban workshops; and finally the preforms were processed by the craftsmen. Quarrying involved excavating shafts into hillsides and removing large chunks of raw material. When these had been brought to the surface, as much of the poor quality cortex or waste material as possible was removed, so that porters needed to carry only usable stone back to the city. The debris from this initial processing still forms solid obsidian mantles hundreds of meters in diameter around the mine shafts. The porters who carried the preforms to Tula probably used baskets borne on their backs and held in place by tumplines. The lack of evidence for permanent Toltec settlements near the mines suggests that the miners and porters visited the quarries several times a year and occupied temporary camps. Upon arrival in the city, the obsidian was taken to workshops where professional knappers lived and worked. The Tula obsidian workshop zone may have covered all of 0.8 sq. mile (2 sq. km) on the east side of the city. We excavated a small testpit in this area and recovered debris from different processing stages and tools which broke during manufacture. Healan's recent excavations in the same general area have confirmed its identification as an obsidian workshop zone but suggest that the workshop occupied a smaller area than our surveys indicated.[11]

The most common items produced by the obsidian knappers were cylindrical or polyhedral blade cores from which prismatic blades were later struck. The cores were prepared by carefully flaking away excess material until the desired shape and size had been achieved. This task required considerable skill because one misdirected blow would ruin the entire block of raw material. After the core was formed, long sharp blades could be removed

fig. 30

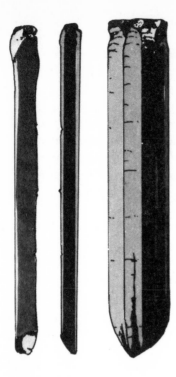

30 *Obsidian blade and core technology. Left, bottom view of a blade; center, top view; right, exhausted core. Length 13.5 cm.*

from it by holding it between the feet and applying pressure with a crutch-like implement held against the chest. Each blade was removed from a spot adjacent to the previous one and the blade maker circled around the core circumference until it became exhausted, i.e., so small that no more blades could be obtained from it. A core yielded 100–150 blades and a skilled knapper could use one up in about an hour. Fresh blades were extremely sharp and maintained their edges for a long time if properly used. Even old discarded blades still hold a surprisingly sharp edge – as most Mesoamerican archaeologists have accidentally discovered from time to time! Almost anything softer than obsidian could be cut with these blades, some of which were hafted into wood handles to form knives. At times they were also set into the edges of wooden swords of the type the Aztecs used so effectively against the Spaniards.

Our evidence suggests that Toltec craftsmen concentrated on producing cores for sale rather than blades. Used-up cores are found all over the city, not simply in the workshop zone, and we recovered enough of them in our excavations to account for all the blades we excavated. Unlike core preparation, blade removal is a relatively simple task almost anyone can learn, and apparently most consumers bought cores and struck off their own blades when they needed them.

Obsidian was also used to make bifacial knives. After the blank was prepared, the artisan pressure-flaked it into the desired shape by detaching small chips with a hand-held flaking tool. Although most bifacial knives served as utilitarian tools, some were used to open the chests of human sacrificial victims prior to removing the heart. Pressure-flaking was also used to produce projectile points, rasps, pulpers, hide scrapers, and eccentrics – the most exotic and problematic of obsidian artifacts found at Tula. Eccentrics are tiny E- and U-shaped objects whose form symbolized water and human blood (i.e. sacred water) in Mesoamerican art. We do not know their function but suspect they were attached to ceremonial costumes or other ritual objects.[12]

It is clear from all this that obsidian was one of Tula's most important industries, though it is difficult to estimate the number of people employed in it. There are several possible methods of arriving at a figure, but all involve considerable guesswork. The most realistic estimate I have come up with is that 2,000 craftsmen could have supplied Tula, the surrounding region, and foreign consumers with cores, bifaces, and other objects. If each worker supported four additional people, (for example a wife and three children), 15,000 people or more than 40 percent of Tula's population depended on this industry for a livelihood.

Commerce

Toltec craftsmen obtained their food and farmers their industrial products through a highly organized market system. We will learn much more about this system when archaeologists identify and excavate the major market place; meanwhile the little we know can be supplemented with historical inform-ation on the famous Aztec market at Tlatelolco, Tenochtitlan's twin city.

Bernal Diaz del Castillo has left us an eyewitness account of the Tlatelolco market in his *True History of the Conquest of Mexico*. According to him it was held in a large building where '. . every kind of merchandise was kept by itself and had its fixed place marked out.'[13] Among the products for sale were metal objects, precious stones, feathers, mantles, slaves, cloth, thread, cacao, ropes, sandals, animal skins, live animals, foods of all sorts, pottery, wood, honey, paper, dyes, and stone tools. Policemen, he reported, patrolled the area and brought people accused of stealing and cheating before judges who sat in session during business hours and passed immediate judgments. The Aztecs used units of measure based on the Mesoamerican vigesimal system, volumes derived from standard-sized containers, and quasi-monetary standard values calculated in cotton mantles or cacao beans.

plate 54

The Tlatelolco market was the largest in a complex system which included local, regional, and major urban markets. The major markets operated daily; the others were conducted periodically on a five or twenty day basis. This ancient pattern was so widespread in highland Mesoamerica at the time of the Spanish conquest that it must have functioned in Toltec times. The main differences between the Aztec and the Toltec system were probably related to size and scale; the Aztec system was much more complex and its major markets far exceeded in size those of the Toltecs because the total population they served was much greater.

Tula's major market certainly offered local, regional, and international products to its clients. Local goods would have included pottery, obsidian, ground stone tools, agricultural produce, river fish, baskets, cloth, and a multitude of other craft products. The surrounding region would have contributed wood, lime, salt, special agricultural products, fish and other lake products from the Basin of Mexico, unusual kinds of pottery, semi-precious stones, wild animals, and animal pelts.

Most of the things the average Toltec family consumed came from nearby but the élite used many items brought from far afield. Rare animal skins, feathers, cotton cloth, metal objects, jewelry, fancy pottery, cacao, tobacco, marine shells, peyote, and hallucinogenic mushrooms were all essentials in the daily and ritual life of the upper class and many came from areas outside the Toltec state.

The importation of these exotic goods was almost certainly controlled by a specialized merchant group similar to the Aztec *pochteca*. The *pochteca* were a quasi-noble group of hereditary merchants who organized expeditions to distant lands in search of valuable and exotic goods. Although formally independent of the government, they acted as spies and agents provocateurs in the cause of Aztec military imperialism. Some journeys took years, allowing time for the armed caravans to trade in the places they visited. They bought goods in one foreign community and resold them at a profit in another, much like modern independent merchant ships which buy and sell cargoes as they move from port to port. Eventually they returned home with valuable cargoes carried by slaves who were sold at the journey's end. Their wealth bought them élite status at home but also aroused jealousy and cupidity in their fellow nobles so they feigned poverty in public and entered Tenochtitlan silently under the cover of darkness. *Pochteca*-like organizations existed as early as Teotihuacan times and the Toltec *pochteca* may have been descendents of Teotihuacan merchants who abandoned that city when its economy faltered.

plates 55, 56

fig. 31

The routes along which the Toltec *pochteca* traveled are not precisely known, but several major ones can be postulated. One extended west through Michoacan to the Rio Lerma-Santiago drainage and followed that river through northwest Mexico to the Pacific coast. A second went north along the eastern foothills of the Sierra Madre Occidental through Zacatecas and Durango into the deserts of northwest Mexico. The most important one led eastward across the mountains into the tropical lowlands. This route provided access to the exotic goods of the Gulf coast and linked Toltec merchants with their Putun Maya counterparts in Tabasco and Campeche. Putun Maya merchants controlled a coastal trade route which followed the shore of the Yucatan peninsula into Central America; they appear to have collaborated with the Toltecs in the conquest of Chichen Itzá and the Yucatan peninsula.

Of the things brought home by the Toltec *pochteca*, only pottery and a few

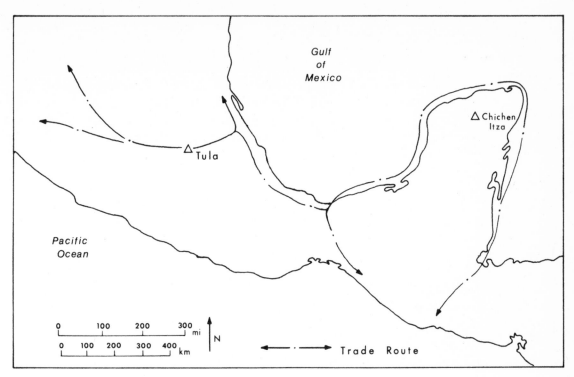

31 Hypothetical routes followed by Toltec merchants.

miscellaneous items have survived in the archaeological record. Cobean identified a number of ceramic trade wares in our collections, including Central American Papagayo polychrome, Plumbate from the Pacific coast, Central Veracruz wares and Huastec pottery from the North Gulf coast.

Plumbate was the most important trade pottery at Tula; in fact, we found more of it than many of the rare locally-made types. Its unique lustrous surface was produced by using special clay slips and firing techniques. Plumbate was popular throughout Mesoamerica for several centuries and the Toltec *pochteca* undoubtedly controlled its distribution in the northern and western regions for at least part of that time. Cacao and green quetzal-bird tail feathers, two other famous products of the Plumbate homeland, were probably imported along with the pottery; indeed the vessels may simply have been saleable containers for more valuable cacao shipments.

The Gulf coast provided many valuable goods in addition to pottery; exotic foods, cacao, cotton, feathers, rubber, and jaguar pelts could all be obtained in this area and the Toltecs may even have imported maize from the nearest tropical territories during bad harvest years in the highlands. Most of the ceramic imports came from the Huasteca area in the north. A few pieces from the Tuxtla mountain region in the south have been identified but the distinctive Fine Orange ware of southern Veracruz, Tabasco, and Campeche is

fig. 32

plates 42, 43, 45

32 *Plumbate turkey effigy vessel.*

conspicuously absent at Tula. This absence is puzzling because Fine Orange was widely traded in Mesoamerica and is almost always found with Plumbate. Hostilities between the Toltecs and the Putun Maya producers of Fine Orange can be ruled out as a factor, in view of their joint conquest venture in Yucatan. Perhaps the Toltecs imported only small quantities of Fine Orange for use by élite families whose houses have not been excavated.

There is good reason to believe that Toltec merchants traveled into the northern desert-steppe lands. This lightly settled zone did not offer many markets; on the other hand it contained valuable minerals and semi-precious stones, such as turquoise, serpentine, quartz, rock crystal, mica, amethyst, and cinnabar. Moreover it was a major source of peyote and hallucinogenic mushrooms used in religious rites. The Pacific coast shells we found in our excavations indicate commercial ties with west Mexican groups in Michoacan, Nayarit, and Colima. Other products, particularly metal ornaments, may have come from this same area. Mesoamerican metallurgy originated in west Mexico after AD 700. The primary emphasis was always on copper ornaments although gold and a few other metals also were worked in small quantities. Whereas archaeologists have never found metal objects at Tula, some of the painted figures on banquet friezes display yellow bracelets and necklaces which I believe were made of copper or gold. I doubt that Tula had any resident metalworkers despite Sahagun's passing references to Toltec metallurgy, so these objects are best explained as trade pieces from the west.

How did the Toltecs pay for their imports and what did they have that other peoples wanted? These questions are difficult to answer because very few *bona fide* Toltec objects have been found at other Mesoamerican sites. One reason for this is that archaeologists have not devoted much attention to sites of this period, another is that many of the Toltec products were perishable and have not been preserved.

The Toltecs probably exported two major classes of goods: obsidian tools and élite craft products. Obsidian was ideally suited for bulk export. Not only were cores and tools light, thus enabling a porter to carry many at a time, but the localized occurrence of obsidian meant that access to it could be monopolized by a strong power, and the potential demand was both large and steady.

Control of the Pachuca obsidian mines and its desired products gave the Toltecs a definite advantage vis-à-vis their competitors. The superior qualities of Pachuca obsidian as a raw material for tools is still an open issue, but the important thing is that ancient Mesoamericans obviously prized it above all others and were eager to obtain it.

The exported craft products were élite goods manufactured at Tula from both local and foreign raw materials. Feather cloaks, headdresses and shields, turquoise mosaics, *tecali* vessels, jewelry, and many other exotic products entered the 'international' trade network after being fashioned in Toltec workshops. Quetzal feathers from Guatemala might be made into an elaborate shield, which was then taken north and traded for beautiful shells from the Gulf of California or raw turquoise from New Mexico. The articles manufactured by the Toltecs were desired not only on account of their beauty and the exotic materials used, but because the symbols on them represented pan-Mesoamerican ideas and beliefs. For example, while a Toltec craftsman may have had very specific ideas about the Quetzalcoatl he painted on a leather armband, the ultimate consumer in highland Guatemala could easily re-interpret it as Gucumatz, his own version of the Feathered Serpent god.

Farmer, craftsman, merchant, warrior, priest, and ruler; each contributed something to the Toltec economy. The pitiful remnants of Toltec civilization today allow us to see only a pale shadow of the system's complexity and integration, but at least we have begun to make some headway toward a better understanding of this important topic.

8 The Toltecs in central Mexico

Up to this point Tula has been our main focus of attention. This chapter concentrates upon the area encompassed by the Toltec state as well as Tula's relationships with its central Mexican neighbors; the next chapter discusses Toltec 'international relationships' with other parts of Mesoamerica. As always there are many gaps, but the documentary and archaeological records tell us enough to allow a coherent if sketchy reconstruction.

The Toltec state

Three obstacles face the scholar who attempts to reconstruct the geographical limits of the Toltec state. First, the written sources do not list the areas which paid homage or tribute to the Toltecs. Second, with the exception of the Basin of Mexico, very few archaeological studies have been devoted to the areas where we believe the Toltecs concentrated their political and military efforts.

The third obstacle relates to the very nature of Mesoamerican states. If the Toltec state was similar to the historically documented Aztec, Tarascan, Oaxacan, and Mayan ones, precise definition of its borders will never be possible. Mesoamerican states did not have well-integrated territories marked by fortifications or other visible markers. They were loosely held aggregations of conquered peoples who frequently rebelled against their masters. The general pattern of state expansion was for an imperial power to co-opt or coerce a local ruler into pledging allegiance and sending periodic tribute to the capital. If he resisted, the province was conquered and a small garrison was stationed there as insurance against revolt. No attempt was made to reorganize the local population and very few physical traces of the conquest were left to enter the archaeological record. The fact that revolts were often successful meant that the area controlled by a conqueror fluctuated from one decade to another.

Tula's short lifespan as a major power meant that its political and military control over neighboring groups was similarly brief. The borders of the Toltec state must have shifted very rapidly, and we cannot detect these shifts in the information at our disposal. Nevertheless we do have some vague ideas about the areas included in the core of the Toltec state or empire.

fig. 33   Several ethnohistorians have attempted to define the limits of this state using information in the Colonial period documents, and their findings more

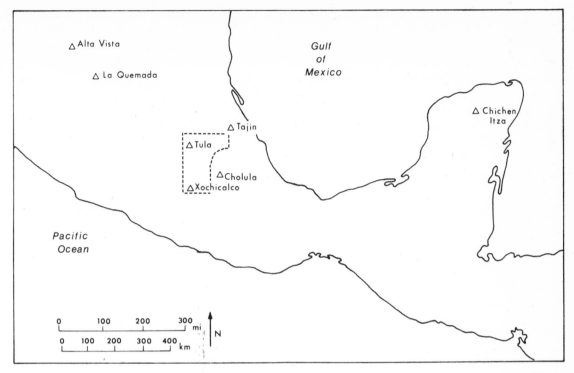

33 *Approximate limits of the Toltec state.*

or less agree.[1] The area they propose includes much of central Mexico and adjacent areas to the north; specifically Hidalgo, the Basin of Mexico, the Valley of Toluca, and parts of the Bajio and Morelos.

The northern boundaries are very uncertain. On the northeast, Toltec control probably extended to the western slopes of the Sierra Madre Oriental mountains; on the northwest it included portions of Queretaro, Guanajuato, Zacatecas, and Michoacan. Most of the northern boundary coincided with the limits of effective agriculture because the Teochichimeca nomads north of this line were too difficult to conquer and the potential tribute was not worth the effort. The eastern, southern, and perhaps western boundaries were primarily determined by the presence of potentially hostile competitor states, i.e. Tajin to the east, Cholula on the southeast, Xochicalco to the southwest, and possibly an incipient Tarascan state to the west in Michoacan.

The basic motivation for Mesoamerican empire building was to acquire 'free' wealth in the form of tribute. Conquered populations were required to send large quantities of local products to their overlords several times a year. We do not know what tribute goods the Toltecs received, but detailed information is available on the later Aztec tribute exacted from the area of the former Toltec state. This information is found in the Matricula de Tributos, a sixteenth-century list of the tribute the Aztecs received from each province in their empire. Although the Aztecs may have required larger quantities and different kinds of goods than did the Toltecs, the Matricula indicates what things were produced in the areas formerly controlled by the Toltecs, as well as the items that at least one conquest state considered desirable as tribute.

Aztec tribute emphasized three classes of goods: staple foodstuffs, textiles and exotic luxury goods. The foodstuffs included maize, beans, chilis, amaranth, chian, and animals. Certain alien foods such as cacao and honey were also collected if possible. The textiles were made of cotton and maguey fiber. The cotton goods were particularly valued and included men's mantles, women's skirts and blouses, and quilted warriors' costumes complete with shields. The luxury goods included feathers, animal skins, minerals, semi-precious stones, and a long list of miscellaneous élite items.

Every Aztec province inside the boundaries of the former Toltec state sent maize, beans, and amaranth seeds to their overlords and I suspect the same was true in Toltec times. These foodstuffs would have been an important supplement to the local Tula area production, particularly in bad years when some tributary areas had better harvests than the arid Tula zone. Most of this food was probably distributed to the craftsmen and other occupational specialists in Tula, although some may have been stored for future emergencies.

The Toltecs must also have held cotton cloth in high esteem, to judge from its prominence in the documentary accounts. The only major cotton source in the Toltec state was the temperate lower part of Morelos.[2] Cotton goods were reserved for the élite in Conquest-period societies and the same was undoubtedly true for the Toltecs.

Miscellaneous goods received by the Aztecs as tribute from the former Toltec area included lumber, pottery, lime, a type of paper made from the inner bark of the *amate* tree, honey, and wild animals. The Aztecs did not acquire feathers, rubber, cacao, precious stones, and exotic animal pelts from this area. This was presumably because such goods did not occur there, the Toltecs probably having obtained them through trade rather than tribute.

The Basin of Mexico

The Basin of Mexico is one of the best-studied archaeological areas of its size in the world. In addition to the numerous excavations conducted there since 1900, the entire Basin has been surveyed by William T. Sanders, Jeffery R. Parsons, Richard E. Blanton and their colleagues since 1960. These surveys located several thousand archaeological sites of all periods in an area of 6000 sq. km,[3] and tell us a great deal about the Basin population during Toltec times. We know how many communities existed, the extent of each, the possible number of inhabitants, and their distribution pattern. The surveys also provide information on the dynamics of culture change; that is, what changes occurred, when and why. Thus we can trace the history of the area

35 Drawing of Toltec pottery by Charnay, who either excavated or purchased these typical but somewhat fancifully drawn vessels during his pioneering explorations in the 1880s.

Local Tula pottery

36 (*Above*) Mazapan Red on Buff bowl, design painted with a multiple brush technique. Ht 13 cm. Possibly from Tula, but exact provenance unknown.

37 (*Below*) Sillon incised tripod bowl, Tollan phase. Ht 8 cm.

38 (*Right*) Tarea polished red miniature jars or goblets, Tollan phase. Ht *c.* 8 cm.

39 Abra coarse brown brazier or *incensario*. The weeping eyes identify the face as that of Tlaloc.

40 Abra coarse brown brazier fragment. A Tlaloc eye found associated with the Canal Locality temple.

41 Aztec pottery found in a looters pit near El Cielito. The pieces on the left are Black on Orange wares, the others are polychromes.

Foreign wares

lumbate effigy jar lid decorated with shell
lay. A bearded man emerges from the mouth
coyote. Found near the El Corral temple.

lumbate effigy jar representing a dog (?).
nd in San Antonio Suchitepequez, Guatemala.
3 cm.

lumbate vessels found in the House II cache,
al Locality. The vessel on the far left has
e balls in the hollow supports, its neighbor is
rd effigy, the others are simple goblets. Ht of
el on the right, 12 cm.

45 Plumbate effigy of a warrior's head, probably broken from the front of a jar. Found in the Canal Locality excavations.

46 Papagayo polychrome vessels found in the House II storage pit, Canal Locality. The goblet served as drinking cups, and the bowl may have been a serving dish. The tallest goblet is 15 cm high.

47 Duplicating ancient pottery. The potter is painting a copy of a Papagayo polychrome goblet as part of the ceramic manufacturing study.

Figurines

48 (*Above left*) Moldmade Mazapan 'gingerbread' figurine. The painted designs on this female (goddess?) are unusually well preserved. Ht 10 cm. Provenance unknown.

49 (*Above right*) Moldmade Mazapan 'gingerbread' figurine from the Canal Locality. One of the very few unbroken samples from the UMC Project excavations.

50 (*Left*) Tollan phase figurine head from the Canal Locality. The goggle eyes and handlebar moustache identify him as Tlaloc.

51 (*Below*) Tiny carved serpentine plaque from the Canal Locality, depicting a man wearing large round ear plugs.

Economic life

54 (*Right*) Model of the Tlatelolco Aztec market. This portion of the mod shows food vendors as described in eyewitness accounts by Spanish Conquistadores.

55, 56 (*Below right*) Sixteenth-centur drawings of Aztec pochteca merchants Note the use of tumplines and backpacks.

52 Woman grinding maize with a mano and a three-legged metate. The shapes of these basic kitchen utensils have not changed for thousands of years. (Cf. plate 33.)

53 Pachuca obsidian mine area. The black material is waste discarded on a talus slope near a mine shaft.

57 Cholula, Puebla. A colonial church crowns the largest earth temple mound ever constructed in the Americas.

58 Airview of Xochicalco, Morelos. This city was protected by its hilltop location and the dry moats and associated embankments visible on the lower slopes. The Temple of Quetzalcoatl is in the center.

Cholula, Xochicalco and Tajin

59 Temple of Quetzalcoatl, Xochicalco. Seated figures occupy the spaces created by the undulations of the Feathered Serpent's body.

60 Temple of the Niches, Tajin, Veracruz. The function of the niches is not known but the total of 365 suggests a calendrical significance.

Chichen Itzá

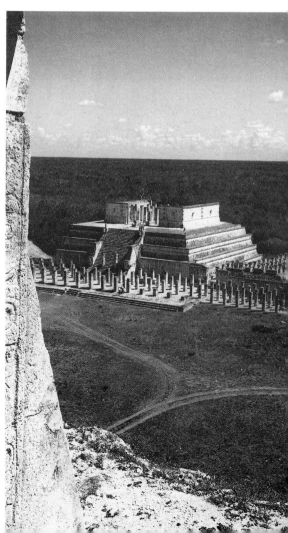

61 (*Top*) Chichen Itzá, Yucatan, from the air. The Castillo is on the left, the Temple of the Warriors on the right. (Cf. fig. 35.)

62 (*Above*) The Castillo, Chichen Itzá. This Toltec-Maya structure was dedicated to Kukulkan, the Maya equivalent of Quetzalcoatl.

63 (*Right*) Temple of the Warriors, Chichen Itzá, view from the Castillo. This structure is a virtual twin of Tula's Pyramid B.

64 (*Top*) West Façade, Temple of the Warriors, Chichen Itzá. Masks of the Maya rain god Chac flank a Feathered Serpent very similar to Tula's Tlahuizcalpantecuhtli.

65 (*Above*) Chac Mool, Chichen Itzá. This sculpture is virtually identical to its counterparts at Tula. (Cf. plate XII.)

66 (*Right*) Square roof supports, Temple of the Warriors, Chichen Itzá. Toltec warriors are depicted on the carved surfaces.

67 Atlantean altar or bench, Temple of the Warriors, Chichen Itzá. Identical Atlantean figures are known from Tula.

68 Ballcourt, Chichen Itzá, looking north. The game could be won in several ways, one of which was to drive the ball through the stone ring near the top of the wall.

69 Tzompantli or Skull Rack, Chichen Itzá. Carved skulls duplicate the real ones mounted on stakes on top of the platform. (Cf. plate 78.)

70 (*Below*) Platform of the Eagles and Jaguars, Chichen Itzá. This structure and the neighboring Venus Platform are probably Toltec Maya analogs of Tula's Adoratorio.

Alta Vista, La Quemada and Casas Grandes

71 Alta Vista, Zacatecas, Hall of the Columns and portion of the Southwest Court. The columns served as roof supports.

72 Votive Pyramid, La Quemada, Zacatelas. This structure at the northern Toltec outpost was apparently truly pyramidal rather than flat-topped with a temple at its summit.

73 Casas Grandes, Chihuahua. View of some of the adobe residences which were occupied at the height of the community's prosperity, around AD 1250.

74 (*Above left*) Sixteenth-century drawing of Quetzalcoatl doing penance by drawing his own blood. Blood-letting of this type was a routine priestly activity. The conical hat, feather device on his back, curved stick, and cut conch-shell emblem are all insignia associated with this god. This and the following two illustrations are from Sahagun's *Florentine Codex.*

75 (*Above right*) Quetzalcoatl bathing at midnight. Spartan activities such as this were common features of a priest's life.

76 (*Below*) Quetzalcoatl in a drunken sleep. The first in a series of disasters which led to his downfall and flight from Tula.

Ritual and myth

77 A sacrifice. The victim is held down by assistants while the priest opens his chest with a stone knife. This and the following illustration are from *Book of the Gods and Rites and the Ancient Calendar* by Fray Diego Duran.

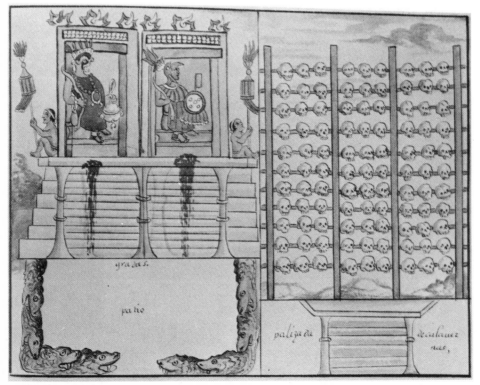

78 Aztec temple and Tzompantli or Skull Rack. The blood on the temple steps is from human sacrifice, the skulls on the rack atop the masonry platform belong to sacrificial victims. (Cf. plate 69.)

from Teotihuacan's decline to Tula's florescence and deduce the impact of the Toltecs on this portion of their territory.

Although Teotihuacan was no longer a pan-Mesoamerican power by AD 800, it remained the largest and most powerful community in central Mexico. At this time it contained 30,000 or 40,000 people living in an area of 1.9–2.3 sq. miles (5–6 sq. km).[4] The population continued to decline as farmers and craftsmen moved out of the city. Many of the emigrants remained in the Basin and established new settlements adjacent to the best agricultural lands. By AD 950 six distinct settlement clusters had arisen in different parts of the Basin; each contained at least one major town and a number of smaller satellite communities. Each settlement cluster may have formed a small independent statelet, although it seems likely that Tula already controlled the northern part of the Basin while Cholula controlled the southern part.

The population dispersion or ruralization which began with Teotihuacan's decline accelerated during the Second Intermediate Phase Two or Tollan phase. The surveys recorded more than 700 sites for this period; 10 towns, 19 large villages, 100 small villages, and 555 tiny hamlets. More than 50 percent of the people lived in small communities with less than 500 inhabitants, a dramatic change from the highly urbanized pattern of earlier times.

The population distribution within the Basin also changed dramatically. The northern third became densely settled for the first time in its history, while the southern section experienced a demographic and cultural eclipse. Furthermore the two zones were separated by a virtually uninhabited east-west strip in the center of the Basin. Some scholars have suggested this empty area was a buffer zone or 'no man's land' between Toltec and Cholulan spheres of influence.[5] This interpretation has been challenged but I find the evidence for it convincing.[6] If the strip was indeed a buffer zone, it is the only definite boundary of the Toltec state identifiable in the archaeological record.

Tula's central Mexican competitors

Tula did not exist in a political vacuum. In addition to the dying Teotihuacan, it had to contend with vigorous competitors in every quarter except the north. Cholula, located east of the mountains which separate the Basin of Mexico from the Puebla valley, was the largest and perhaps most important of these. Most of the investigations at the site have concentrated on the famous pyramid which today supports a beautiful Colonial church. Almost nothing is known about the rest of the pre-Columbian settlement. Cholula was a major center during the Middle and Late Horizons but its status in the intervening 500 years is not clear. Some evidence suggests it remained a major center during this period although it may have been smaller than in earlier and later times.[7]

plate 57

If Cholula was a power during the Second Intermediate period, the two basic bones of contention between it and Tula would have been control of the Basin of Mexico itself and the trade and communication routes leading from it to the Gulf coast. Cholula sat astride one of these routes while the other lay in territory definitely controlled by the Toltecs. Toltec-Cholulan relationships may not have been entirely antagonistic since several documentary accounts refer to cooperation between the two or at least between the Cholulans and one Toltec faction. Quetzalcoatl and his supporters are said to have fled to Cholula after being forced out of Tula, and ethnohistorian John Mulloy has suggested that the Toltec and Cholulan dynasties maintained close relationships and perhaps even an alliance for a time.[8] Obviously much more research is needed before we really understand the situation, but one thing is certain: Cholula outlived Tula by centuries and was the scene of a major battle during Cortes' conquest of Mexico.

Xochicalco was Tula's second major central Mexican rival in early Toltec times. The city was located on several hilltops near the Morelos-Guerrero border. Large fortifications in the form of ditches and ramparts provide mute testimony to the troubled times of Xochicalco's florescence. The site's occupational history is still unclear but it apparently emerged as a regional center while the area was under strong Teotihuacan control or influence.[9] This area was probably a key element in Teotihuacan's imperial design, because it produced cotton and other semi-tropical products not grown in the Basin. It also provided access to sources of jade, serpentine, and other minerals in the Guerrero mountains and marine products from the Pacific coast.

plate 58

Xochicalco grew as Teotihuacan declined and may have contributed to the latter's troubles by gaining control of the Morelos-Guerrero resource area. It reached its peak between AD 600 and 800 when the Temple of Quetzalcoatl, the ballcourt, a palace-like élite residence, and the fortifications were constructed. The city went into an abrupt decline after AD 800 and was abandoned within a century. The reasons for this are not known: Tula or Cholula may have cut it off from vital trade partners or resource areas, or perhaps internal factors led to its demise. If the Toltecs did not contribute to Xochicalco's problems, they certainly took advantage of the situation by establishing trade connections and perhaps exercising actual political control in the Morelos cotton zone.[10]

plate 59

The situation confronting Tula on its western border is not clear. The Tarascan state which blocked later Aztec expansion in that direction was only a century or two old and remains of earlier states have not been identified in the area.[11] Little is known of this part of Mesoamerica, however, and it may contain many archaeological surprises, including remains of a Second Intermediate period polity comparable to Xochicalco. The large archaeological site of Teotenango, recently excavated by Roman Piña Chan may have been the capital of just such a state, but it is too early to tell.[12]

To sum up: the central Mexican heartland provided the Toltecs with virtually all the basic resources they needed. Foodstuffs, fibers, obsidian, basalt, construction materials, wood, lime, and other necessities were available in quantity within a three or four day walk from Tula. This resource base was absolutely essential for the growth and maintenance of a healthy Toltec state and as long as they controlled it, the Toltecs flourished. When the situation changed in the twelfth century, Tula and its inhabitants experienced a rapid decline. Before we go into that aspect of Toltec history, however, we should examine their relationships with more distant neighbors in other parts of Mesoamerica.

9 Toltec contacts with Greater Mesoamerica

The Toltecs lived in a turbulent era which offered them many opportunities for economic and military expansion. This chapter examines their complex relationships with distant contemporaries outside central Mexico. It has to be admitted that the available information is limited and at times contradictory. Nevertheless the main outline of events is fairly clear. The Toltecs were imperialists motivated by economic goals which they attempted to achieve through a combination of political and military means, and their brief but spectacular career as an imperial power set the pattern for later Aztec ventures along the same lines.

The new order in Mesoamerica

Mesoamerican societies experienced drastic changes after AD 700. The new political, economic, and social systems which emerged remained viable for the remainder of the pre-Columbian era even though the political fortunes of individual societies waxed and waned at a rapid pace.

The new age began with Teotihuacan's decline; Monte Alban and the Maya centres in the southern Mesoamerican lowlands followed within a century or two. The relationship between events in the Basin of Mexico and those elsewhere is confused, but Teotihuacan was Mesoamerica's largest and most powerful empire prior to the Aztecs, and its collapse must have had a substantial impact on its neighbors. However, the fact that the other civilizations did not follow suit immediately suggests that they survived this initial shock and later succumbed to difficulties of a more local nature.

The changes in Mesoamerican life at this time involved much more than mere shifts in political fortunes; settlement patterns, art styles, architecture, economics, and religion all show signs of significant change. Many communities which had existed for centuries broke up and new ones arose at different locations. These changes involved villages and hamlets as well as administrative centers. Some communities were established on hilltops and other easily defended sites; others were where they could control agricultural land, irrigation water, communications routes, raw materials or other important resources. Only in the very unusual case of the Maya was an entire realm covering several thousand sq. km almost completely abandoned and never reoccupied.

Domestic architecture did not change much, at least as far as we can tell, but a host of new élite architectural features appeared. These included I-shaped ballcourts with carved stone rings mounted on the walls, rectangular colonnaded halls with large interior rooms and benches, carved serpent column doorways, square platforms in plaza centers, and skullracks. Many of these new features were reflections of the religious changes going on at the time.

New cults, or new variations of old ones, grew in popularity. Quetzalcoatl's prominence increased tremendously, particularly in his guises as the Feathered Serpent and Ehecatl, the Wind God. Tezcatlipoca and a number of other gods whose cults can be traced to the north grew in importance, as did human sacrifice and death symbolism. The new art styles were permeated with military themes such as the eagle and jaguar warrior societies, armed men, and battle scenes.

All these features were present at Tula and in some cases they appeared elsewhere as a result of Toltec contacts. Since the specific nature of the contacts varied from one area to another, the best way to approach the topic is to examine each region in turn.

Oaxaca

Oaxaca has been the homeland of Zapotec, Mixtec, and other Indian groups for several millennia. The Valley of Oaxaca in the central part of the state was the focal point of cultural developments until about AD 750, when it was eclipsed by the Mixteca Alta zone to the north. Monte Alban, the largest ancient settlement in the Valley, was the Zapotec capital during the First Intermediate period and Middle Horizon. This city of 20,000 or 30,000 people occupied a hill which dominated the surrounding valley floor.[1] The hilltop was covered with a large plaza containing temples, palaces, a ballcourt, and other public buildings. Zapotec sculptures at Monte Alban and nearby San José Mogoté contain the oldest known examples of writing in Mesoamerica.[2] Many of the texts apparently commemorate military victories over neighboring villages and clearly indicate the antiquity of organized warfare in Mesoamerica. The hillsides below the plaza are covered with terraces which originally supported houses.[3] Each small terrace or group of terraces was occupied by a family or a few related families. The commoners who lived here farmed the fields in the valley below, manufactured craft products, and served the élite.

Carved inscriptions at Monte Alban suggest that the rulers maintained friendly commercial ties and political alliances with Teotihuacan.[4] Under these circumstances it is not surprising that the latter's decline adversely affected the Monte Alban Zapotecs. We do not know when Monte Alban was abandoned; it seems to have prospered for a time after its ties with Teotihuacan were broken but then declined and was soon deserted. Most of the population had probably moved to other parts of the Valley of Oaxaca by AD 800. No evidence of violence or conquest has been found at the site; apparently the buildings were simply left as the inhabitants moved out.

Mixtecs living in the Mixteca Alta had gained political and economic sovereignty over much of highland Oaxaca by the time Tula became a major power. Although most Mixtec archaeological sites are small compared to other Mesoamerican ruins, Mixtec craftsmen produced some of the finest jewelry, ceramics, and feather objects ever made by American Indians.

The Mixtecs forged a large political state only once in their history. This occurred under the leadership of Eight Deer, a famous eleventh-century ruler from Tilantongo, whose exploits are described in several Mixtec codices. These pictorial books provide long dynastic histories of local ruling lineages and some contain references to Tula and the Toltecs.[5] One authority maintains that the Tula they refer to was actually Tilantongo rather than Tula, Hidalgo, but this interpretation has not received much support.[6] John Mulloy, another student of the codices, believes that Mixtec and Toltec rulers established close ties by means of alliances, marriages, joint military ventures, and co-rulerships of some territories.[7] Although I find this interpretation more plausible than Chadwick's, I am frankly puzzled by the lack of archaeological evidence for such ties.

The Gulf coast

The Gulf coast has more large archaeological sites than virtually any area in Mesoamerica. Despite these archaeological riches, very little work has been done there and the pre-Columbian cultures are still obscure, although we do know that the cultural and political leadership of the area gravitated progressively northwestward. The south coast area was preeminent during Early and First Intermediate times, then control shifted to the large Middle Horizon center at Matacapan in the Tuxtla mountains. Matacapan was a major Teotihuacan colony or ally, and served as a key control point in the lowland trade route followed by Teotihuacan merchants.[8] The center flourished for a short time after the Teotihuacanos withdrew but was soon replaced by Tajin, a large Second Intermediate period center located in central Veracruz.

Tajin was initially settled during the First Intermediate period. It attained regional importance during the Middle Horizon and became a major Mesoamerican power after Teotihuacan's decline. The famous Temple of the plate 60 Niches apparently was constructed in the sixth century; other major buildings erected in the succeeding centuries include the Tajin Chico palace, the Building of the Columns, several temples, and many ballcourts, including the well-known South Ballcourt with its marvelous carved panels.[9]

Jose Garcia Payon, the Mexican archaeologist who excavated at Tajin for many years, was of the opinion that the site was occupied until about AD

1100.[10] I believe it was abandoned before this, but until we know for certain I must assume that Tula and Tajin coexisted and shared a frontier somewhere in the Sierra Madre Oriental mountains. The apparent absence of evidence for contact between the two centers suggests that they did not maintain friendly relationships.

The Huasteca zone north of Tajin's realm was an area of special interest to the Toltecs. The best evidence for this is found in the documentary sources but archaeological remains indicate it as well.[11] Unfortunately the information is so fragmentary that the specific nature of the contacts is not very clear.

Several myths dealing with the origins of the Toltecs state that they first landed on the Huasteca coast and roamed about in the lowland area several years before coming to Tula.[12] The accuracy of these accounts is difficult to assess; they may be sheer fantasy or may refer to a small group of migrant craftsmen or other specialists who eventually found a congenial home in the growing Toltec metropolis.

Both the archaeology and the documentary sources suggest a strong Huastec impact on Toltec religion and ritual. The Corral temple is the most clearcut archaeological evidence we have of this influence. It was almost certainly dedicated to Ehecatl, the Wind God. Round temple bases are rare in Mesoamerica but the Huastecs adopted them as a preferred architectural form early in their history and the entire Ehecatl cult is generally attributed to them. On the other hand at least one authority on west Mexican archaeology has suggested that the cult and its associated architecture originated in that area, so perhaps the case for a Huastec origin is still open to question. We had hoped to uncover evidence of Huastec or other foreign residents in our Corral Locality excavations but aside from a few pieces of Huastec trade pottery, nothing we found indicates the ethnic affiliation of the occupants.

The documentary sources credit the Huastecs with introducing various cults and religious practices at Tula but do not mention the Ehecatl cult. One of the rituals they do describe is the arrow sacrifice associated with the Huastec goddess Tlazolteotl, in which the hapless victim was tied to a wooden rack and shot full of arrows by dancing priestesses. Another is the grisly Xipe Toltec ritual where the unfortunate victim's skin was flayed from his body and worn by a priest. If these practices were in fact introduced by the Toltecs, I suggest they were carried out at the Corral temple rather than in the Tula Grande area.

Sixteenth-century writers claimed that the Huastecs played a major role in the Toltec downfall. According to one of the more esoteric accounts, the god Tezcatlipoca, having disguised himself as a Huastec chili vendor at Tula, created one calamity after another until Quetzalcoatl and his followers were obliged to leave the city.[13] This legend and others like it can hardly be accepted as true history but when combined with the rest of the evidence, they suggest very close ties between groups in the two areas.

We find scattered signs of Toltec trade and contact at several sites in the Huasteca. A few ceramic types in the Tampico area and elsewhere closely resemble Tollan phase materials and Toltec-like architecture can be seen at Castillo de Teayo and other sites.[14] Much more evidence of this sort should appear when archaeologists eventually work on the Huasteca.

Our knowledge of Toltec contacts with the area south of Tajin is equally fragmentary. Earlier Olmec sites have received the lion's share of archaeological attention, very little being known about the later cultures. The Villa Alta phase occupations at sites in the Coatzacoalcos river basin belong to this period but unfortunately a few pieces of Plumbate Pottery are the only indications of Toltec contacts.[15] Our Tula ceramic collections contain pottery from the Tuxtla mountains northwest of the Coatzacoalcos river and although a few Toltec or Toltec-inspired vessels have been found in that area, the significance of these scattered finds is not clear. The ethnohistorical accounts contain several ambiguous references to relationships between the Toltecs and the south Gulf coast and some scholars believe the Nonoalca immigrants at Tula came from there.[16] Our ignorance about this area is particularly regrettable since it formed part of a larger border zone including Tabasco and Campeche which figured prominently in the Toltec contacts with Yucatan and the Maya area.

The Maya lowlands

Oddly enough, the farther from central Mexico one goes, the better the evidence becomes for Toltec contacts. The best evidence is found in Yucatan, where archaeological remains and local historical traditions indicate conquest by a group of Toltecs or other Mexican peoples under strong Toltec influence. The invaders established their capital at Chichen Itzá and controlled most of northern Yucatan for a century or two. In order to understand these events we should first briefly examine Maya history during the preceding period.

The southeastern Mesoamerican lowlands were the homeland of Classic Maya culture, one of America's most arresting pre-Columbian civilizations. Its origins extended back into the pre-Christian era, but it reached its zenith during the Second Intermediate period, by which time the Maya numbered millions. In AD 800 the Maya area contained numerous independent states, although many of the smaller ones may have been loosely allied or affiliated with large centers such as Tikal, Copan, and Palenque. Each state had a 'capital' which contained temples, palaces, ballcourts, and other public buildings. Whilst the élite lived in these communities along with their retainers, the urban status of Maya centers is the subject of much spirited debate. Most Mayanists argue that they were true cities but some of my colleagues and I are not convinced, since they lacked the dense settlement, town planning, complex institutions, and imperialistic successes normally associated with true urbanism. Even if the Maya were not an urban society, their achievements in architecture, art, calendrics, writing, and astronomy were impressive, to say the least.

After AD 800 the Maya experienced a time of unprecedented difficulties which culminated in the abandonment of much of the area by the end of the ninth century. Construction ceased at major centers, existing buildings were allowed to deteriorate, carved monuments were no longer erected, and the inhabitants began to move away. The splendid seats of Classic civilization were soon covered with dense jungle and even the villages and hamlets were deserted. The depopulation of such a vast area makes the Classic Maya collapse a very unusual phenomenon; many other civilizations have declined and abandoned their major centers but something far more serious and permanent must have occurred in the Maya case.

Although many explanations have been offered for the Classic Maya collapse, the causes still elude us.[17] Civil wars, invasion, disease, natural disasters, climate change, agricultural over-exploitation, and environmental degradation have all been suggested, but valid objections can be raised to every single-cause hypothesis proposed so far. In all likelihood a variety of factors were at work and the immediate causes, while related in some form to overpopulation and environmental difficulties, varied from place to place.[18]

The collapse did not affect all parts of the Maya lowlands to a like extent; in fact, northern Yucatan subsequently experienced a belated florescence. This zone was somewhat peripheral to the southern Maya core area in terms of cultural developments prior to AD 700. After that time Uxmal and other centers in the Puuc hill area of western Yucatan began to grow in size and importance. They continued to thrive for a time after the collapse to the south but apparently were abandoned by AD 1000. The reasons for their demise are not known but may be related to Chichen Itzá's rise as a conquest state.

We are fortunate to have historical records for northern Yucatan extending back to about AD 900. The two principal sources of information are the writings of Bishop Diego de Landa and the books of Chilam Balam. Landa was a Franciscan missionary who studied Maya history and life and recorded what he learned in a manuscript called La Relacion de las Cosas de Yucatan, a document as valuable in many ways as that of his Franciscan colleague Sahagun.[19] The books of Chilam Balam are several manuscripts containing the prophesies of a Mayan priest of that name living at the time of the Spanish conquest.[20] According to Ralph Roys, a leading modern student of Maya ethnohistory, the partially Christianized Colonial Maya guarded these manuscripts from Spanish eyes for centuries, and the existing documents are seventeenth- and eighteenth-century copies of older originals which no longer exist.

The Maya believed that time was cyclical and that things which happened in the past were destined to be repeated in the future; therefore, those who knew the past could accurately predict the future. Hence the Chilam Balam manuscripts contain a great deal of useful information about the pre-Columbian period. Unfortunately several obstacles face modern scholars who attempt to use them. First, they are very fragmentary and incomplete. The pre-

Columbian Maya recorded their history and many other things in codices, but virtually all of these were destroyed by the Spaniards in their evangelical zeal to stamp out the old pagan religion. Ironically, Bishop Landa was one of the most avid burners of codices because he considered them an important element in the native religion he wanted to eradicate.

The second obstacle is that the Maya calendar used in the books is difficult to correlate with ours and in many cases the dates given in them cannot with confidence be assigned to specific years or even centuries. Finally, the prophesies and other Colonial writings in the Yucatec Maya language are often phrased in metaphors which cannot be understood today; in fact, at times they make the Biblical Book of Revelations sound like a straightforward newspaper account by comparison! Despite these difficulties, Roys, J. Eric S. Thompson and others have assembled an account of Yucatecan history which correlates well with the archaeology of the area.

The story opens with an invasion of Yucatan by the Maya-speaking Putun, who lived on the western edge of the Maya territory in modern Tabasco and Campeche. Their sixteenth-century descendants were notable maritime merchants who controlled the rivers and coasts of the area and moved goods from the Gulf coast to the Bay of Honduras by canoe. The ninth-century Putun took advantage of the unsettled conditions around them and began to spread out from their homeland. They conquered and occupied Seibal, a classic Peten center for a short period before it was abandoned, and also established more permanent control over the Yucatan coastal trade route. Using Cozumel Island on the east coast of Quintana Roo as a base, they marched inland and conquered Chichen Itzá from the east. The reason for choosing this circuitous route rather than coming directly from their homeland is not clear, but the more direct route may have been blocked by Uxmal. After establishing their capital at Chichen Itzá, they soon subjugated most of northern Yucatan. The name Chichen Itzá means 'at the rim of the well of the Itza'. The Yucatecan natives called the invaders the Itza and the well referred to is the Sacred Cenote, a large natural sinkhole where the water gods were thought to live. The Itza language differed only slightly from Yucatec Maya but their dress, weapons, religion, architecture, and economic activities all reflected considerable acculturation to central Mexican norms.

A second group of conquerors appeared on the scene at Chichen Itzá in AD 987. Their leader was named Kukulkan, the Yucatec word for Quetzalcoatl or Feathered Serpent, and everything about them suggests direct ties with the Tula Toltecs.

Archaeological investigations at Chichen Itzá and other Yucatecan sites confirm and amplify this sketchy historical outline. Two basic periods have been defined at Chichen Itzá; a pre-Toltec phase with Puuc style architecture similar to that of Uxmal and other western Yucatan sites, and a Toltec-Maya phase when Tula architecture and art forms were faithfully copied. The first phase lasted from about AD 900 to 1000, the second from 1000 to 1200 or 1250.

Buildings of the first phase are concentrated in the southern part of the site *figs 34, 35* far from the Sacred Cenote. They include the Nunnery, Iglesia, Caracol, and other smaller structures. Most authorities consider them poorly executed imitations of the 'real' Puuc style but they do indicate that Chichen Itzá was a major power in northern and central Yucatan at this time.

The area near the Sacred Cenote is called New Chichen Itzá because the *plate 61* buildings there belong to the more recent Toltec-Maya period. Although this zone was the core of the community after AD 1000, Toltec-Maya structures are found scattered throughout Old Chichen Itzá as well. The best known buildings of this period include the Castillo, Group of the Thousand Columns, Temple of the Warriors, Ballcourt, Tzompantli, Venus Platform, Eagles and Jaguars Platform, as well as the Balankanche cave. All except the cave were concentrated around a large open plaza connected to the Sacred Cenote by a raised causeway, or *sacbe*.

The plaza is dominated by the Castillo, the tallest ancient building in this *plate 62* part of Yucatan. This square temple pyramid has nine terraces and stairways on all four sides. The temple faces north and consists of a central sanctuary surrounded by interior galleries. Landa says that the Castillo was dedicated to the god Kukulkan, and feathered serpent columns supporting the door lintel *fig. 36* support his statement. The doorjambs and pillars inside the temple are covered with carvings of Toltec warriors. The Castillo visible today encloses an older, slightly smaller structure which is virtually identical to it. Excavations in the temple of this older building uncovered a Chac Mool and a beautiful stone jaguar carved in the round. The jaguar is painted red and its spots are represented by inlaid jade disks. Its position in the temple suggests it was a throne, and mural paintings on the nearby Temple of the Warriors show Toltec warriors or priests seated on similar thrones. The Chac Mool's function is not known but I suspect that it was used as an altar for holding offerings or other objects.

The Group of the Thousand Columns and the Temple of the Warriors fill the east side of the plaza. The Group of the Thousand Columns contains several colonnaded halls facing a large interior courtyard. Its layout is very similar to that of the entire Tula Grande Plaza and the colonnaded halls with their decorated interior benches were clearly copied from Tula prototypes.

The Temple of the Warriors is a stepped platform mound supporting a *plate 63* masonry temple. Sculptured and painted panels showing eagles and jaguars devouring human hearts are to be seen on the platform walls while carved and painted depictions of Chac, the Mayan water god, and Quetzalcoatl decorate the temple exterior. Sculptures of feathered serpents with their chins resting on *plate 64* the ground and their tails high in the air frame the temple doorway. Toltec warriors are shown on the carved stone columns which supported the temple *plate 66* roof and they appear again as miniature Atlantean figures supporting a small *plate 67* altar in the back chamber. All these motifs except the Chac masks are identical to pieces at Tula. An older structure called the Temple of the Chac Mool lies

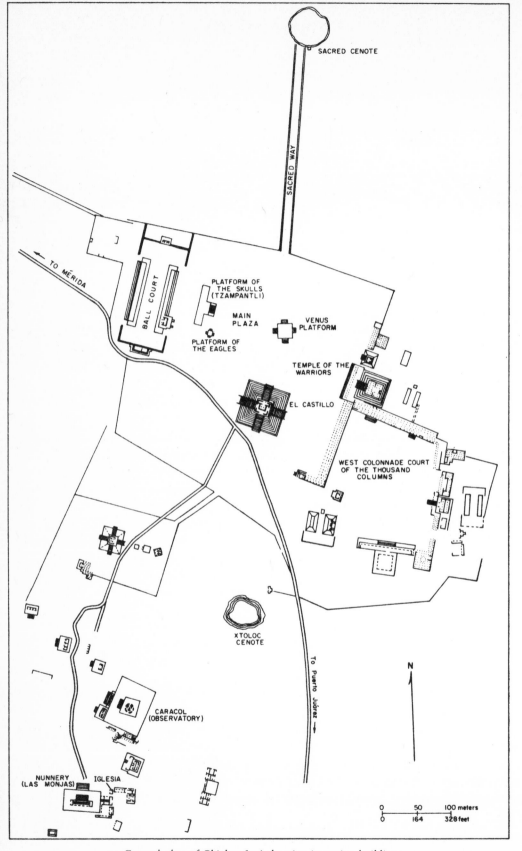

SACRED CENOTE

SACRED WAY

TO MÉRIDA

BALL COURT

PLATFORM OF
THE SKULLS
(TZAMPANTLI)

MAIN
PLAZA

VENUS
PLATFORM

PLATFORM OF
THE EAGLES

TEMPLE OF THE
WARRIORS

EL CASTILLO

WEST COLONNADE COURT
OF THE THOUSAND
COLUMNS

To Puerto Juárez

XTOLOC
CENOTE

N

CARACOL
(OBSERVATORY)

NUNNERY   IGLESIA
(LAS MONJAS)

0   50   100 meters
0   164   328 feet

34 *Ground plan of Chichen Itzá showing its major buildings.*

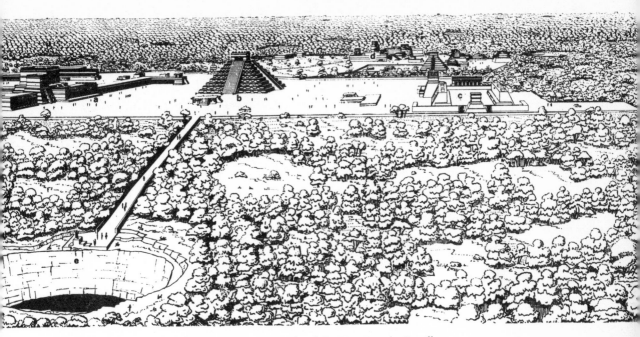

35 Reconstruction drawing of Chichen Itzá. a, Temple of the Warriors; b, Castillo; c, Ballcourt; d, Caracol; e, Sacred Cenote.

beneath the Temple of the Warriors; the name refers to a chac mool sculpture found on the temple floor. Both buildings are clear copies of Tula's Pyramid B, albeit with the addition of minor Maya features such as the Chac masks.

plate 65

The ballcourt at the west end of the plaza, the largest known in Mesoamerica, is a typical Toltec or central Mexican structure. The features it shares with Tula ballcourts include an I-shaped ground plan, stone rings mounted high on the center walls, and temples overlooking the playing field. Sculptured panels on the playing field walls depict ritual scenes, including the beheading of a ball player, perhaps the captain of a losing team. The Temple of the Jaguars overlooks the southeast side of the ballcourt. It is a typical Toltec structure with feathered serpent doorway sculptures. The interior temple walls were covered with elaborate painted murals which were copied in the early twentieth century before they faded. Arthur Miller, having recently studied these copies, concluded that the murals depicted a series of battles between the armies of two commanders he calls Captain Serpent and Captain Sun Disk.[21] Captain Serpent's symbol is a feathered serpent, and although Miller suggests that the battles occurred near Seibal in the Peten, they may in fact depict the Itza conquest of Yucatan.

plate 68

The Tzompantli or Skull Rack is a low platform east of the ballcourt. It seems identical to the largely destroyed Tzompantli Matos recently excavated at Tula. The platform sides are covered with grisly carved stone panels

plate 69

showing human skulls strung on upright posts like beads on a necklace. These probably symbolize the real skulls which once covered the platform summit.

plate 70   The Venus Platform and the Platform of the Eagles and Jaguars are small flat structures analogous to the Tula Grande Adoratorio. Both have stairways on all four sides. The Venus Platform is decorated with feathered serpents, Kukulkan-Quetzalcoatl figures, and symbols of the planet Venus; the Platform of the Eagles and Jaguars shows feathered serpents and the familiar Toltec birds and felines eating human hearts. Balankanche is a spectacular limestone cave located a few miles east of the Castillo. Subterranean passages connect several large chambers where the ancient Maya placed offerings in shallow pools of water. The offerings include Toltec style braziers decorated with Tlaloc faces and Toltec warriors; a few are so similar to Tula pieces that they may be imports from there.[22]

Chichen Itzá's foreign overlords ruled Yucatan for about two centuries. A triple alliance involving Chichen Itzá, Mayapan, and Uxmal is said to have governed the area near the end of this period. Mayapan was a growing settlement at this time, and the fact that Uxmal had already been abandoned for several centuries is just one of the puzzling contradictions in the story.

The account of Chichen Itzá's downfall at about AD 1200 is recorded in considerable detail and is worth repeating here because it offers a fascinating glimpse into the machinations of pre-Columbian politics and illustrates one way in which Mesoamerican centers lost their power and status.

A Mayapan ruler named Hunac Ceel was the main actor in the drama.[23] According to one version of the epic as reconstructed by Roys, Hunac Ceel was a minor noble who achieved fame with a dramatic act at Chichen Itzá's Sacred Cenote. It was the custom of the time to cast precious jewelry and other objects into the cenote as offerings to the water gods. In times of drought, humans too were thrown in as offerings and as messengers who were supposed to plead the people's case before the gods living in the cenote. Victims who survived the fall from the cenote rim to the water 20 m below were expected to obtain a prophesy and repeat it after being hauled back up.

On one occasion, Hunac Ceel is said to have attended a ceremony in which all the messengers died and he saved the day by jumping in to obtain the prophesy himself. His deed supposedly earned him the rulership of Mayapan, but he wanted to rule all of Yucatan. So he first attacked and destroyed Chichen Itzá. The reason for his 'treachery', as it is referred to in the accounts, was to avenge an insult to his ally, the ruler of Izamal. Chichen Itzá's ruler had abducted the bride of the Izamal groom during the wedding ceremony, and Hunac Ceel responded by helping Izamal attack and defeat Chichen Itzá. He then turned on Izamal, defeated his former friend, and seized control of the entire peninsula.

After their defeat the Itza fled south into the wilderness around Lake Peten Itzá in Guatemala. They established a new capital at Tayasal, an isolated settlement where they maintained their independence, warding off first

Mayapan and later the Spaniards, until AD 1696. Although Chichen Itzá was never reoccupied, the Sacred Cenote continued to attract pilgrims bearing offerings to the water gods well into the twentieth century.

The historical and archaeological evidence for Toltec rule at Chichen Itzá raises a series of unanswered questions. Who were the invaders and where did they come from? What role did Tula and the central Mexican Toltecs play in the affair? Was Kukulkan the Ce Acatl Topiltzin Quetzalcoatl who fled Tula? What kinds of relationships did Tula maintain with Chichen Itzá's Toltec rulers? What effects did the conquest have on the native Maya?

The answers to these and other questions will only come after much more research is done. It may be prudent to avoid speculation on them but I prefer to abandon caution for the moment and offer a few tentative suggestions.

The Putun identity of the conquerors is generally accepted but could be strengthened if we knew more about the archaeology of their homeland. The first wave of invaders were already under strong Toltec influence and the second may have been led by true Toltecs from Tula. This may or may not imply direct involvement by Tula's rulers. Perhaps Toltec merchant-warriors were the main agents, advising their Putun allies or manipulating events behind the scenes. It may even be that the Toltecs were a dissident faction who broke away from Tula and established their own independent state. This proposition is supported by one interpretation of the central Mexican legends, though it is far from proven. However, if it is true, it would explain the apparent absence of Yucatecan products at Tula. On the other hand the two centers may have maintained an active trade which simply does not come to light in the archaeological record. Salt, honey, slaves, and perhaps cloth were major Yucatecan exports in the sixteenth century; slaves and cloth would not leave any traces while salt and honey may have been shipped in perishable containers. It is also possible that many non-local items such as Plumbate and Papagayo pottery were transhipped through Yucatan.

The architectural and stylistic similarities between Tula and Chichen Itzá are so strong that they suggest a close and enduring relationship. These two sites are closer to being carbon copies of each other than any other Mesoamerican communities at any time, a fact which certainly suggests direct control from Tula.

Who was Kukulkan? We seem to be dealing with both a god and a human being named after him, but that is about all that can be said at the moment. Arthur Miller's Captain Serpent may be an important piece in this puzzle but it

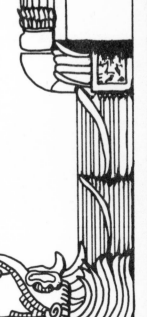

36 Carved stone feathered serpent doorjamb, Chichen Itzá.

is too early to tell. The scholar who unravels the mystery surrounding the identities of the various Quetzalcoatls and Kukulkans will cut the Gordian knot of Mesoamerican studies; in the meantime I doubt that Kukulkan was the same Quetzalcoatl who fled Tula.

Whilst some of the effects of the Toltec conquest on the native Maya are apparent, many more are likely to be discovered in due course. Toltec names, gods, and rituals were permanently established in the culture of the élite, but the impact on the peasantry is not known. There seems to be a consensus of opinion among Mayanists that peasant life was left unaltered by the conquest but future investigations in village sites may change this impression.

The Maya highlands and adjacent Pacific coast

Histories of the Quiche, Cakchiquel, and other highland Maya groups written in the Colonial period contain numerous references to Toltecs and the Toltec ancestry of the ruling dynasties. Unfortunately archaeological investigations have not confirmed these contacts. Central Mexican influence is evident in both earlier and later times but not during the Second Intermediate period. Ethnohistorical investigations by Robert Carmack suggest that the 'Toltec' migrants arrived in the area from Chichen Itzá or perhaps the south Gulf coast after the collapse of Tula and may thus have claimed more Toltec ancestry than they actually merited.[24]

Despite the lack of evidence for direct Toltec contacts with the Guatemalan highlands, there are indications of commercial ties, however indirect, between the two areas. The quetzal feathers so highly prized by the followers of Quetzalcoatl could only have come from this area, the bird's only known habitat. Also, the large quantities of Plumbate pottery at Tula may have arrived there *via* highland Guatemalan intermediaries. The trade in these exotic goods was presumably routed through Putun merchants in Tabasco and Campeche, and perhaps even through Chichen Itzá.

Northern Mexico

Until about twenty years ago we knew virtually nothing about northern Mexico in pre-Columbian times. This state of affairs has changed dramatically since 1960 thanks to the efforts of Pedro Armillas, Charles DiPeso, J. Charles Kelley, Phil C. Weigand, and a few other scholars. The excavations and surveys done by this small band of people, who realize that civilizations cannot be understood without knowledge of happenings at their peripheries, have provided us with a fascinating picture of what occurred pre-Hispanically in this area.[25] Weigand has summarized much of this research in several recent articles on which I have drawn extensively.[26]

plate 71   Alta Vista, Zacatecas has been the focal point of investigations by Kelley, Weigand, and their colleagues. This Mesoamerican frontier settlement was initially occupied during the First Intermediate period. At about AD 350 Teotihuacanos or their representatives took control of it and embarked on a major program of construction, colonization, and economic exploitation.[27] Their interest in this distant area was due to the presence of exotic minerals such as malachite, cinnabar, hematite, limonite, colored chert, galena, and rock crystal in nearby gravel deposits. The Alta Vistans may have mined these minerals before the Teotihuacan intrusion but the operations were greatly expanded after they took control.

Mines consisting of large caverns connected by narrow passages were excavated with the use of handtools. The extent of the mines is staggering; at least 750 were opened up over a period of four centuries. Mining must have been an uncomfortable and dangerous occupation; smoke from the pine torches, oppressive heat, poor ventilation, physical exhaustion, and the ever-present danger of cave-ins were just a few of the unpleasant features of an Alta Vista miner's life. Weigand suggests that the rulers used coercion to make the miners work and I cannot help but wonder if the latter were not slaves. Certainly the archaeological remains at the ceremonial center suggest a harsh and oppressive society with much more regimentation than was found at Teotihuacan and other contemporaneous centers in Mesoamerica.

The lack of evidence for craft workshops suggests that the minerals were exported to Teotihuacan for processing. Presumably Teotihuacan artisans used them for manufacturing élite goods, which were consumed in the city or exported to other consumers.

After a century or two the Alta Vistans learned about large turquoise deposits far to the north in what is today New Mexico. They began to send out expeditions which mined this valuable blue-green stone and brought it back as raw material. Workshops for processing turquoise were established at Alta Vista where beads, tiny chips for mosaic elements, and other articles were produced by local craftsman. More than 17,000 turquoise fragments have been found at Alta Vista, many in workshop contexts, an indication that as the local mining industry declined, turquoise replaced it in the economy.

Alta Vista's prosperity is reflected in its material remains; according to Weigand it contained among other things 'a solstitial observatory, a turquoise workshop; a Hall of Columns; small pyramids facing enclosed courtyards, at least one of which was a palace; elegant burials, one series in a crypt; a skull rack.'[28] I have already discussed the fact that some Alta Vista architectural features such as colonnaded halls and skull racks appear to be prototypes for later structures at Tula. Other notable features shared by the two sites include skull portrayals in art, human sacrifice, and cannibalism. These common features in later Mesoamerican societies were not typical when they first appeared at Alta Vista. If art reflects ideology and social realities, as is frequently the case, Weigand probably is correct in viewing Alta Vista society as an oppressive colonial enterprise whose primary motivation was profit from labor intensive mining and exotic resource extraction.

Alta Vista did not suffer an immediate crisis when the Teotihuacanos withdrew from the area, perhaps because it found new clients for turquoise at Cholula, Xochicalco, Tajin, and elsewhere. However, the site and its hinterland were abandoned soon after AD 900. There are several possible reasons for this: although the mines were not worked out, the craftsmen may have been cut off from their turquoise supply. Some of the people moved north into Durango, others went south toward the Mesoamerican heartland. Some of the latter probably settled at Tula but others may have stopped at La Quemada in the Rio Malpaso valley, Zacatecas, where they became the ancestors of the Caxcanes and other historic period Indian groups.[29]

plate 72

The fortress community of La Quemada was located several hundred km south of Alta Vista. The Rio Malpaso valley was a marginal area until the Toltecs or their allies established a garrison at La Quemada around AD 900. The site's fortification and setting on a steep hill make it one of Mesoamerica's most impressive military complexes, truly a 'castle-town' to use Pedro Armillas' term.[30] In addition to the defensive walls, there are temples, a ballcourt, a colonnaded hall, what may be military barracks, and an extensive network of roads connecting it with outlying settlements in the valley.

Weigand believes that La Quemada was a major control point along an inland trade route which extended north from central Mexico to the turquoise sources at Chaco Canyon, New Mexico, USA. Archaeologists working at Chaco Canyon have identified a dramatic set of culture changes involving turquoise mining on an unprecedented scale during this period. Local Anasazi Indians probably consumed much of the turquoise, but some was traded south into Mesoamerica.[31] I suspect that much of the precious green stone was sent to Tula where it was either used or re-exported to still other consumers. Two spectacular turquoise-inlaid plaques at Chichen Itzá provide a good example of the complex trade network involved here. Both were obviously made by central Mexican craftsmen, perhaps Toltecs living at Tula. Whilst the source of the turquoise used in them has not been positively identified, the New Mexico mines, located more than 2800 miles (4600 km) away, are the most likely place of origin.

Who built and occupied La Quemada? It could certainly have been the Toltecs, for the site was located near the borders of their realm and was occupied during Tula's florescence, but the Caxcan Indians are the most likely candidates. They were an agricultural Chichimec group mentioned as Toltec allies in some of the historical sources, and their descendents still lived in the area when the Spaniards arrived. The local indigenous inhabitants under their control apparently included the ancestors of modern Tepecano and Hichol Indians.

Whoever ruled La Quemada must have acted in a very harsh fashion. Three lines of evidence support this contention: the need for fortifications, the violence which caused it to be abandoned, and folktales about the downfall of the town that have been handed down. La Quemada means 'the burnt place' in

Spanish, and every excavation done at the site shows it was thoroughly sacked, burnt to the ground, and never reoccupied. This event could be explained by either a conquest or a rebellion, but Weigand has collected modern myths from Huichol Indians which suggest the latter.

According to one version of the myth, an evil priest lived on a great rock surrounded by walls and covered with buildings. Eagles and jaguars under his command compelled the inhabitants to pay a tribute in peyote and also prevented them from going to the coast for feathers, salt, and shells. As a result the people could not make proper offerings to their gods, and the corn crops failed. The gods advised them to remedy the situation by going to the evil priest's abode. When they arrived the jaguars attacked them but the sun god destroyed the jaguars and their malevolent leader with twenty days of heat. The eagles were away on patrol at this time; on their return, they attempted to locate the rebels but failed to do so and left the area. Thereupon the corn grew once again and the people could obtain salt, feathers, and shells. The gods warned them never to return to the rock because of the evil associated with it.[32]

Weigand believes that the legendary fortified rock was La Quemada and the evil priest its ruler. The eagles and jaguars probably represent warrior societies, perhaps Caxcan equivalents to élite Toltec squadrons. The disruption of trade by the overlords may have been an attempt to gain control over the distribution of peyote and the other products. The solar heat which destroyed the site and its inhabitants seems to be a metaphorical allusion to the fire which destroyed the site. Divine warnings not to return to the great rock have been honored ever since; La Quemada was never reoccupied and even today the Huichols swing far north of it on their annual peyote-collecting trek to the desert, even though this adds days to their foot journey.

The final northern site involved in our story is Casas Grandes, Chihuahua. Despite its location far north of the Mesoamerican border, Casas Grandes was a trade and manufacturing center having strong ties with central or west Mexico.[33] The site has a long history, but the Medio period (1060–1340) was the time of its florescence. Prior to this it was a small village similar to many others in northern Mexico and the southwestern United States. Then a sudden, massive influx of Mesoamerican ideas and traits changed virtually every aspect of Casas Grandes life. The new features included the feathered serpent cult, ballcourts, the siting of buildings around courtyards, ceramic decorations, and an entirely new economic orientation. The former agricultural way of life was replaced by a marked emphasis on manufacturing and trade. DiPeso and his colleagues found Medio period workshops with thousands of debris fragments and finished products, mostly ornaments of various sorts. Whilst shells from the Gulf of California were the most common raw material, copper, turquoise, rock crystal, specular iron crystals, and other rare minerals and stones were also utilized. Featherworking was another important craft at Casas Grandes and the excavators uncovered remains of imported exotic birds such as scarlet and military macaws as well as aviaries where they were kept.

plate 73

Casas Grandes products were traded north to Arizona and New Mexico and south into central and west Mexico.

This desert emporium prospered for about 200 years but stagnation and decay set in during the middle of the thirteenth century. The community continued to function at a reduced level until its destruction at about AD 1350, when it was attacked and burned, the slaughtered inhabitants being left unburied where they fell. Apparently the attackers were not interested in looting, for they left a wealth of valuable objects behind. DiPeso suggests they were local area residents who simply wanted to end the tyranny of the Casas Grandes overlords.

How did Casas Grandes relate to the Toltecs? DiPeso believes that much of the Mesoamerican contact and influence in the Medio period can be traced to Tula, a supposition I find difficult to accept. Tula was already on the wane when the period began and even if the Toltecs provided the initial impetus, other groups had to replace them as consumers after Tula's collapse. Theoretically Casas Grandes could have been ruled by former north Mexican allies of the Toltecs who broke away or were cut off from Tula but the evidence at hand does not support this idea. I suspect we will someday learn that Casas Grandes' major markets were located in Michoacan, Jalisco, and other parts of west Mexico rather than Tula.

We are now in a position to form a reasonably coherent picture of northern Mexican prehistory and its Toltec and other Mesoamerican relationships, even though our information is still very fragmentary. The first farmers entered the area from the south, searching out the limited areas with enough moisture and good soil for maize agriculture. Most of the small villages they established were physically and socially isolated from the mainstream of Mesoamerican civilization but certain places such as Alta Vista began to exploit minerals and other exotic resources which could be traded to the south. After AD 350 these resources attracted the attention of central Mexican imperial powers who established colonies and outposts in order to guarantee delivery of the exotic goods. Turquoise and other rare materials were the major products which interested them because they were valuable enough in small quantities to pay the expense and effort of maintaining outposts thousands of miles from the homeland.

These exotic raw materials were not basic essentials of life in the sense that maize, pottery and obsidian were, but they did play a vital role in the urban economies of Teotihuacan and Tula. Processing them into finished products generated large profits. Of these profits a certain proportion went directly to the élite but some of the proceeds could be invested in basic foodstuffs from the rural hinterlands, thus insuring an adequate flow of provender into the cities. Robert Santley has recently postulated that the Teotihuacan obsidian industry functioned in this manner, and I believe the same was true of élite industries as well.[34] In fact obsidian tools probably were one of the products exported by Teotihuacan and Tula to the northern colonies in return for the minerals.

Both Weigand and DiPeso suggest that life in the northern colonial societies was quite harsh and oppression a major means of social integration. Apparently people had to be forced to gather shells and turn them over to a tribute collector, or work in the mines, perhaps because their rulers lacked any positive inducements acceptable to the commoners. (This often applies to pre-modern extractive economies and even forms a common thread in the industrial era histories of coal fields in my native Pennsylvania, copper mines in the western United States, and South African diamond mines.)

Although the north Mexican mining and trade centers maintained constant contact with the central Mexican cities, the degree of control exerted over them by the latter is not known. We might expect it to have fluctuated considerably with time and place. In any case, the outposts could not have survived without the southern markets for their products. Alta Vista may have been much more independent of Teotihuacan than La Quemada was of the Toltecs, while Casas Grandes was probably the most independent of all, at least in the political if not the economic sense.

Weigand shows that this colonial economy reached its maximum scope and intensity under the Toltecs. The vastly increased exploitation of the New Mexico mines and the infusion of Mesoamerican cults and motifs into new areas provide good evidence for his contention. It is also reflected in the entire orientation of Toltec culture. The northern immigrants who figured prominently in the Tula population would have been familiar with their homeland's resources and the kinds of management and organization needed to extract them. Teotihuacan had demonstrated the profitability of this kind of economy, so it was natural for the Toltecs to follow the example. Perhaps one of the original motivations for the southward migrations to Tula was to seize control of the entire resource processing economic system rather than serve as a peripheral element in it.

Mesoamerican ties with the north slackened when Tula fell but were not severed until the thirteenth or fourteenth centuries. The reason for the final break are not known; they probably included political instability in central Mexico, Teochichimecan attacks on the caravan routes, and a number of local problems in northern Mexico. The Aztecs probably knew about the northern resources but by the time they acquired the organizational capabilities to reestablish the connections, their Tarascan neighbors stood in the way. If the Tarascans were not strong enough to expand very far northward or perhaps lacked the interest, at least they did block the Aztecs. It is interesting to speculate on what might have happened had the Spaniards arrived a century later than they did. Would the Aztecs have conquered the Tarascans and reopened the north or would the Tarascans have established themselves as the new Toltecs of the north? Obviously nobody can tell. What in fact happened is that both civilizations fell to the Spaniards who quickly moved north and established a new but equally oppressive mining economy based on silver instead of green stones.

10 The demise of the Toltecs

Toltec power and culture came to a catastrophic end in the latter part of the twelfth century when famine, rebellion, and chaos replaced the growth and prosperity of the previous two centuries. By AD 1200 Tula was a ruined shell of its former self and the Toltecs had dispersed all over central Mexico. This chapter is concerned with the Toltec collapse and the factors behind it. First we will look at a native account recorded by Sahagun, then the scanty archaeological information will be reviewed. Next we will examine two syntheses of all the available information; one was proposed by Nigel Davies in his recent book *The Toltecs Until the Fall of Tula*, the other is my own reconstruction. The chapter ends with a brief glance at Tula in post-Toltec times and the special role it played in the Aztec world.

The Toltec collapse is described in several historical sources. The stories vary and frequently contradict each other because the accounts are based on different historical traditions and all probably contain later modifications and embellishments. Furthermore the Mesoamerican penchant for cloaking mundane history in myth was never given a freer rein than in the telling of the Toltec disaster; in fact, some of the accounts are comparable to the Odyssey in their narrative power as well as their credibility.

Sahagun's version

The account we find in Sahagun is one of the most mythical to have been preserved. His informants attributed the Toltec collapse to an epic conflict between cosmic forces personified by the gods Tezcatlipoca and Quetzalcoatl. The Mesoamerican cosmos was often portrayed as a duality symbolized by Quetzalcoatl (good, day, light, and established élite religion) in opposition to Tezcatlipoca (evil, night, darkness, and sorcery). In the Toltec drama, Tezcatlipoca was played by himself, and a priest or ruler named Ce Acatl Topiltzin Quetzalcoatl represented the divine Feathered Serpent. Huemac, a Toltec ruler who may have shared sovereignty with him, also appears.

The fable's basic theme is that Tezcatlipoca created so much misfortune among the Toltecs that they all perished or fled Tula. In the words of Sahagun's informants, 'A great mockery was made of the Toltecs, since the devil had slain very many of them. It is said in sooth he made sport of the Toltecs.'[1]

The living Quetzalcoatl was famous for his life of virtue, chastity, sobriety, and ritual penance. In the opening scene Tezcatlipoca disguised himself as an elderly healer who tricked Quetzalcoatl into drinking pulque to cure an ailment. One drink led to another and soon our paragon of virtue was drunk as the proverbial lord. At that point many of his disgusted followers deserted him. Tezcatlipoca then turned his malevolent attentions towards Huemac. First he appeared naked in the Tula marketplace disguised as a Huastec chili vendor. Huemac's virtuous daughter fell in love with the stranger and implored her father to allow them to marry. He reluctantly agreed, but his followers were so angered by the scandalous affair that he decided to send his son-in-law into a battle from which he would not return. According to Huemac's plan, the Toltec warriors were to abandon Tezcatlipoca to the enemy with only a cadre of dwarves and hunchbacks for support. When the plan was put into operation Tezcatlipoca defeated the enemy and the Toltecs had to accept him as a hero. During the victory celebration he sang magic chants which caused many Toltecs to lose their wits, fall into canyons, and turn to stone. Next he took the form of a valiant warrior and slew more Toltecs in hand-to-hand combat. Then he sat in the marketplace holding a dancing miniature figurine in his hand. Many onlookers were trampled to death as they tried to get close enough to view this marvel. Next he persuaded the Toltecs to stone him to death as a sorcerer; they were only too happy to oblige him, but the odor from his decomposing body caused additional deaths throughout the land. The Toltecs tried to remove the body but it became extremely heavy and many people were crushed to death when the ropes they were using to pull it broke. After this Tezcatlipoca cast a series of spells which made people uneasy and led some to offer themselves as sacrificial victims. His final deed was to turn the foodstores sour and have an old woman toast maize, filling the land with its aroma. The hungry Toltecs came from far away to get the maize but she killed them when they approached her.

Quetzalcoatl and Huemac realized that all was lost and each decided to flee. Quetzalcoatl destroyed his temples constructed of gold, coral, feathers, and other precious substances; changed the cacao trees into mesquite bushes; and drove away the birds with precious plumage which had inhabited the land. Then he left Tula accompanied by his remaining followers and wandered through foreign lands, including Cholula, until reaching Tlapallan on the Gulf coast. There he fashioned a raft of serpents and according to Sahagun, set off across the sea. Other accounts say that he burned himself in Tlapallan and rose from the ashes to become Venus, the Morning Star. Huemac fled to Cincalco, a cave in Chapultepec hill in the Basin of Mexico, where he lived out his days.

The archaeological record

Archaeological findings at Tula verify the fact that the city met a violent end; they do not tell us much about what actually took place or why. Acosta uncovered evidence of fire and destruction in every building he excavated at Tula Grande. Unfortunately he paid only scant attention to the detailed stratigraphy in the soil levels above the Tollan phase structures and failed to recognize the complex sequence of events reflected in these upper levels. Although some of the destruction he noted undoubtedly occurred at the time of Tula's collapse, much of it took place in later times. The evidence for this is clear in Acosta's reports but its significance is not brought out.

Acosta accepted Jimenez Moreno's date of AD 1170 for Tula's collapse. This date is based on information contained in the historical sources and although the correlation of the native dates with our own calendar is still not completely resolved to everyone's satisfaction, most authorities accept Jimenez Moreno's interpretation. Hopes that our excavations would provide additional inform-ation on the subject of Tula's collapse were not fulfilled. Our radiocarbon dates indicate that the Canal Locality houses were abandoned as much as a century before this occurred. It would appear therefore that the urban peripheries were abandoned before the central core of the city and that Tula's decline was a long process rather than a sudden cataclysmic event.

Much remains to be learned about the process of Tula's decline. How rapidly did it occur? What factors caused it? Why couldn't the Toltecs reverse the trends which must have been evident to them? Davies has attempted to outline the events which led to the collapse and to answer some of the questions posed above, so let us now examine his reconstruction of the situation.

Explanations of the Toltec collapse

The scenario Davies proposes is based on documentary accounts and archaeological facts. His sequence of events is as follows:

1 The northern Mesoamerican frontier gradually shifted southward through time, opening Tula to attack in the twelfth century. The initial attack occurred in about AD 1120 and caused some Toltecs to migrate southeastward into lands claimed by Cholula.

2 Immigrants from the northern frontier zone who had settled within the borders of the Toltec state turned on their hosts and answered Cholula's call for help against the Toltec intruders. One group, led by Mixcoatl, 'Cloud Serpent', eventually settled in the Basin of Mexico after helping the Cholulans.

3 In AD 1166 Mixcoatl's son Ce Acatl Topiltzin gained control of Tula and the Toltec throne. He assumed the title Quetzalcoatl and became the Ce Acatl Topiltzin Quetzalcoatl of Toltec history and legend. Tula enjoyed a brief renaissance under his rule but his success bred conflicts between his followers and the traditional Tula-born faction led by Huemac. Increased pressures from the Huastecs and northern Chichimecs (who were farmers rather than true nomadic Teochichimecs) triggered the downfall of both men and each fled to a different part of the Basin of Mexico.

4 Toltec power and civilization ended by AD 1179 and most of Tula's inhabitants moved to various parts of central Mexico.

If this reconstruction is correct, as I believe it to be, what basic cultural processes led to these events? Davies, Pedro Armillas, and others have dealt with this issue, and all seem to agree on certain points which I will take into account in my reconstruction.

I believe the Toltecs were faced with internal problems and external threats which they could neither control nor resolve. The major internal problems were subsistence difficulties and a poorly integrated social system, the external threats came from enemies in several directions. We will consider each of these factors in turn.

Subsistence agriculture has always been a precarious enterprise in the arid Tula area. Low rainfall and broken topography limit the amount of arable land and normal fluctuations in annual precipitation cause more bad years than good ones. Irrigation was as essential in the past as it is today but the technology involved was very different. These days water is stored behind large dams and raised to the level of the fields with mechanical pumps and long canal systems. In addition, the never-ending flow of water from the Mexico City waste disposal system supplements the limited amount of local water. None of these features was available to the Toltecs. For them dry years meant total crop losses on unirrigated fields and river levels which were so low that water could not be drawn off into the canal systems. A single bad year caused hunger; several in a row could easily create famine. The Toltecs faced this problem all along, but it became more critical as the population grew. Although the government undoubtedly sponsored construction of irrigation systems, the size of the irrigated area was constrained by the available moisture and hilly terrain. The productivity of the Tula area in poor years must have placed rather a low ceiling on the carrying capacity, i.e., the number of people who could be supported by the area on a long-term basis. I suspect that the Tula area became overpopulated in this sense by AD 1100, although I cannot prove it.

At this point the skeptic may reasonably ask several questions. Why did the Toltecs not construct dams and reservoirs for water storage or import food from surrounding areas in bad years? The answer is that they did not do so because they lacked the technology to dam up the large fast-flowing rivers of the region. Even the small arroyos could not have been successfully controlled because flash floods which follow the torrential summer storms would have destroyed the dams in a few minutes. Furthermore, the absence of waterwheels and other devices for lifting water out of its natural courses made its storage for irrigation of elevated fields impossible.

The Toltecs certainly depended on imported food for some of their supplies. Some of the imports were in the form of tribute from conquered provinces, the rest were purchased with urban craft products. Nevertheless they faced two grave problems in this regard. Their transportation system was rudimentary and expensive, and the areas they controlled were not particularly productive. The absence of wheeled vehicles and draft animals meant that all transportation had to be accomplished with human bearers or canoes. Aztec human bearers called *tanemes* normally carried loads of about 23 kilos (50 lbs) a distance of 19 miles (30 km) a day, and the same was probably true of the Toltecs. In addition to the relatively small load, the bearers had to be fed cultivated foods while on the road. According to William Sanders and Robert Santley, bearers consumed too much food to make the journey worthwhile if they were on the road more than five days or travelled more than 94 miles (150 km).[2] The Toltecs had very few really good agricultural zones within a five-day walking distance from Tula. Whilst the Basin of Mexico was the most productive area within this radius, Cholula may have controlled the most fertile southern section of it throughout much of Tula's history.

The historical accounts contain many references to food shortages and famines, references which are often coupled with allusions to conflicts and battles over farm land and food stores. For example, several battles are said to have occurred at Xochitlan, a village near Tula with permanent springs close by. Mastache has shown that these springs were used for irrigation in Aztec times and perhaps earlier.[3] Hence conflict over irrigation water and the produce from critical areas in difficult times was to be expected.

In addition to the normal problems of agriculture in this area, the Toltecs may have been exposed to relatively small but very significant climate changes. Pedro Armillas has suggested that northern and central Mexico experienced a phase of decreased summer precipitation at this time.[4] The reduced rainfall would have created serious problems in marginal arid areas such as the Tula river valley and surrounding zones by making rainfall agriculture much more tenuous than before and lowering river levels. Unfortunately we do not have good studies of the ancient climate with which to prove or disprove this attractive hypothesis. Armillas based his argument on the premise that climatic changes documented elsewhere in the world indicated similar changes in northern and central Mexico. This proposition was reasonable at that time but paleoclimatology is a complex subject and we now know that climate changes in one area do not necessarily imply changes elsewhere. Thus we need studies of the climatic history of the Tula area before we can accept drought as a factor in the Toltec collapse.

The second major internal problem the Toltecs faced was a breakdown in social integration. The Tula population was a heterogeneous mixture of people from different areas perhaps speaking several languages. Multi-ethnicity of this sort was common in ancient Mesoamerican cities; urban centers attracted people with many backgrounds and skills and formed them into a cohesive social unit. The Toltec population included people from the Basin of Mexico, the Gulf coast, and various parts of northern Mexico. The Toltecs seem to have successfully integrated these diverse elements early in their history, though the documentary sources suggest severe ethnic conflict near the end of the Tollan phase. The Tezcatlipoca-Quetzalcoatl saga discussed above can be interpreted as a power struggle between a northern faction identified with Tezcatlipoca and an older established Nahuatl-speaking group under Quetzalcoatl's banner. There is also evidence for a group of Huastec speakers associated with Quetzalcoatl as Ehecatl, whose sympathies seem to have lain with the northerners.

What caused this disintegration? I suspect that whatever cohesiveness the Toltecs achieved initially was later strained by economic difficulties including subsistence problems and the loss of markets for manufactured goods. When these problems arose, people took sides based on ethnic affiliations and their leaders were unable or unwilling to share power, wealth, and opportunity with others. The continual flow of migrants into the city further hampered effective social and economic integration. In order to understand how and why this happened, we must first examine the external problems facing the Toltecs.

The Toltecs were confronted by two major external difficulties; the southward retraction of the Mesoamerican frontier, and competition from neighboring states. The changes in the location of the northern frontier were part of a long and poorly understood process which began during the Middle Horizon and was still continuing at the time of the Toltec collapse. The factors which caused it are unclear and probably varied as time went on; it seems likely, however, that climate change, local northern political events, and repercussions from the rise and fall of central Mexican states all played a role.

The climate change theory is attractive even though it remains unproven. If precipitation did decrease in northern Mexico, the effects on agriculture and settled village life could have been disastrous. Consecutive years of poor harvests would have forced farmers either to emigrate or to adopt a nomadic hunting and gathering lifestyle. The wealthy and relatively well-watered lands to the south would have attracted people even if those areas were experiencing the same kinds of difficulties. In addition the later migrants would have been joining predecessors with whom they shared cultural, linguistic, and economic ties. If climatic deterioration peaked after AD 1000, the Toltecs may have faced the prospect of hosting the largest number of migrants in their history when they were least able to do so because of their own subsistence problems.

Agricultural difficulties were only one of the factors prompting southward treks by frontierspeople; shifts in mining and trade patterns suggest other economic difficulties as well. The causes of these changes are likewise unclear, though exhaustion of raw materials was obviously not a factor. Rebellions of the type which devastated La Quemada and Casas Grandes may have been common occurrences if the northern rulers were as oppressive as Weigand and DiPeso suggest. Perhaps the rebels achieved freedom at the price of economic chaos which forced at least some of the people to emigrate.

The unsettled conditions in the north created two problems for the Toltecs. First, the migrations introduced unwanted groups of foreigners into the Toltec heartland. Immigration was not a new phenomenon at Tula but the Toltecs' ability to absorb outsiders diminished as their difficulties grew. Although the immigrants probably arrived in small groups and their total numbers may not have exceeded a few thousands, their wanderings must have turned them into battle-hardened veterans. Whatever their original occupations, they soon learned that wielding a sword or bow was easier and more profitable than farming. These refugees-turned-mercenaries probably offered their services to the highest bidder and often turned against the Toltecs just as Mixcoatl had.

In addition to the problem created by the immigrants, the northern chaos cut off the Toltecs from exotic raw materials and markets for their manufactured goods. Although northern societies accounted for only a small percentage of Tula's trade volume, the loss of access to the exotic raw materials found there had a substantial impact on Toltec politics and alliances. Mesoamerican alliances were fragile arrangements often maintained only as long as both parties benefited. Junior allies expected gifts of exotic jewelry, costumes, and other élite goods in addition to military support from their patrons in exchange for their loyalty. The fact that the Toltecs could no longer provide any of these must have made their allies ponder the wisdom of the arrangements and served as a stark indication of growing Toltec weaknesses. The absence of garrisons and large standing armies made defections easy, particularly since other potential patrons such as the Cholulans were always available. The loss of allies had both military and economic repercussions. Former friends became enemies, former markets for obsidian and other craft products were closed to Toltec merchants, and each loss created favorable conditions for new disasters. Within a few generations the Toltecs will have found themselves surrounded by hostile neighbors on all sides.

Cholula may have been Tula's primary rival in central Mexico. Mixcoatl allied himself with the Cholulans and according to one tradition his son went to Cholula after fleeing the Toltec capital. Cholula had much to gain from the Toltec collapse; access to the rich Morelos cotton lands, uncontested control of the Basin of Mexico, and freedom from Toltec competition for its own obsidian industry were only a few of the potential benefits.

Huastecs and other Gulf coast inhabitants may also have contributed to Toltec difficulties. Some of the groups were Toltec allies at one time but the tenor of the relationship seems to have changed near the end. Control of the Pachuca obsidian mines was one obvious bone of contention between the two groups. There is no evidence that the Huastecs wrested control of the Pachuca mines from Tula, though this may in fact have happened. Such a takeover would have had a devastating effect on the Toltec economy. Unemployed craftsmen would have posed a threat to internal stability and created a further drain on the limited stores of foodstuffs. Also, the imported foods purchased with obsidian tools would no longer have been available. The only real option open to the craftsmen was emigration to Cholula and other cities where they could be sure of obtaining employment and a steady supply of raw materials.

The Tarascans west of Tula may have posed an additional threat to the Toltecs. The Late Horizon Tarascan state based at Tzintzuntzan did not emerge until post-Toltec times but it may have had predecessors we do not know about.[5] Even though very little archaeology has been done in the Tarascan homeland, there are several hints of strong interaction with the Toltecs and we have reason to believe that part of the area was under Toltec control at one time. The loss of control over this area would have cut off the Toltecs from the Zinapecuaro obsidian source, access to the Pacific coast lowlands, and markets for Toltec products.

No single factor was sufficient in itself to cause the Toltec collapse but their simultaneous occurrence after AD 1100 initiated a chain reaction in which each new problem compounded the effects of the others until even a Toltec Solomon could not stop the process of decline. Wise leadership in the early phases might have reversed the process but even if this had happened, the success would only have been temporary. I do not view history as a predetermined, mechanical chain of events, but I do believe that all complex human societies contain structural features and patterns of behavior which eventually become the seeds of their destruction. They also contain the building blocks for future societies and civilizations. The Toltecs were a segment of the culture history of the Mexican people. In a metaphorical sense they accepted the cultural heritage of their predecessors, modified it into a new way of life and passed it on to the Aztecs, who repeated the process. Netzalhualcoyotl, 'Fasting Coyote', an Aztec philosopher-king who ruled Texcoco, is credited with a poem which speaks about men but applies equally well to civilizations. Eric Wolf chose it as an introduction to *Sons of the Shaking Earth*, his classic book on Mesoamerican civilization. I find it a fitting epitaph for the proud and resourceful people who created Toltec culture.

> All the earth is a grave and nothing escapes it;
> nothing is so perfect that it does not descend to its tomb.
> Rivers, rivulets, fountains, and water flow,
> but never return to their joyful beginnings;
> anxiously they hasten to the vast realms of the rain god.
> As they widen their banks, they also fashion
> the sad urn of their burial.
> Filled are the bowels of the earth with pestilential dust
> once flesh and bone, once animate bodies of men
> who sat upon thrones, decided cases, presided in council,
> commanded armies, conquered provinces, possessed treasure,
> destroyed temples,
> exulted in their pride, majesty, fortune, praise, and power.
> Vanished are these glories, just as the fearful smoke vanishes
> that belches forth from the infernal fires of Popocatepetl.
> Nothing recalls them but the written page.[6]

Tula in the Aztec world

Whether or not Tula was completely abandoned at the end of the Tollan phase, we know that it was soon reoccupied. By the time of the Spanish conquest it was a large city once again and although no longer the center of an empire, it played a very unusual role in the Aztec realm. The Aztecs thought of it as the birthplace of civilized life and much of their cultural heritage. They tried to identify with their putative Toltec ancestors by expropriating Toltec art and religious objects for their own use and intermarrying with the local ruling families in the Tula area who claimed legitimate Toltec descent. Tula even remained important for a time after the Spanish conquest, as is evidenced by its handsome Early Colonial church and convent. The river junction on the valley floor replaced the ridge top as the center of the Colonial town, later renamed Tula de Allende, and has remained the focal point of the community ever since.

What is the evidence for Tula's special role in the Aztec world and how can we explain it? Archaeological deposits and written records both provide partial answers to these questions, so I shall examine each in turn.

As indicated above the extent to which Tula was abandoned at the time of the Toltec collapse is not clear. Acosta found Aztec II style pottery above the Tollan phase deposits at Tula Grande. The timespan of this ceramic style is not well documented but most authorities assign it to the thirteenth century. Its presence at Tula can be explained in two equally plausible ways. A remnant Toltec population may have continued to live in the decaying ruins, or immigrants from the Basin of Mexico homeland of Aztec II pottery may have reoccupied the site shortly after the Toltecs left.

Cobean has applied the name Fuego phase to the time of the Aztec II occupation. The virtual absence of Fuego phase ceramics from our urban zone survey collections suggests that the resident population was quite small and lived in and around the Tula Grande plaza. The looting of Toltec art objects probably began at this time and in fact may have been the principal interest of the people living there.

The Palacio (AD 1300–1521) and Tesoro (AD 1521–1600) phases are defined on the basis of changes in Aztec ceramic styles. It is difficult to separate the two in many instances because the Spanish conquest which marks the dividing line between them did not have an immediate impact on native pottery designs and manufacturing techniques.[7] Fortunately we have architectural and historical information which aid us in this regard.

fig. 37 By the time of the Spanish conquest Tula had reemerged as a substantial city. The surveys of Stoutamire and Yadeun suggest that it covered at least 3 sq. miles (8 sq. km). It is difficult to estimate the number of inhabitants because we do not know how densely the area was settled, but I would put it at a minimum of 20,000. Whereas in earlier times this would have been an unusually large city, central Mexico experienced an almost unprecedented

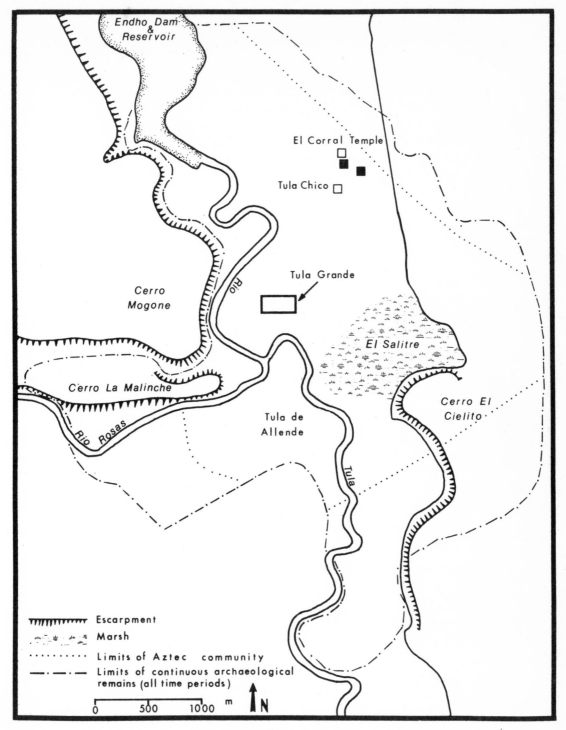

Endho Dam & Reservoir

El Corral Temple

Tula Chico

Tula Grande

Cerro Mogone

El Salitre

Cerro La Malinche

Cerro El Cielito

Río Rosas

Tula de Allende

Tula

Río

Escarpment

Marsh

Limits of Aztec community

Limits of continuous archaeological remains (all time periods)

0   500   1000   m

N

37 Map of Tula in Aztec times.

population explosion after AD 1300 and many communities had surpassed Tula's size by AD 1521.

Some archaeologists believe that Tula Grande functioned as the Late Horizon civic precinct, but I question this. In the first place the Aztecs systematically looted Tula Grande and I doubt whether any local ruler would have been willing to use such a devastated area as his seat of power. Furthermore, Acosta and his assistant Hugo Moedano excavated what was almost certainly an Aztec ruler's palace on El Cielito hill several km southeast of Tula Grande.

Acosta found evidence for Aztec looting in every building he investigated at Tula Grande. They removed virtually every carved stone from the building facades, hewed into Pyramids B and C in order to construct ramps for lowering the heavy carved stone roof supports, dismantled the Adoratorio, and probably dug holes wherever they suspected the presence of offerings. They also erected a few crude platforms in front of Pyramid C, and inside Ballcourt I and the Palacio Quemado, as well as depositing caches of pottery and flint sacrificial knives at various places. Several of these caches were placed on the exposed core of Pyramid C after the facing stones had been removed. The caches were probably ritual offerings made by looters attempting to atone for their desecration of hallowed ground.

Although the looting may have been instigated by local Toltec rulers for their own benefit, most of the objects were ultimately reused in Tenochtitlan and other major Aztec cities. One case in point is a carved stone Toltec bench frieze similar to those in the Palacio Quemado, which was found years ago near the main temple in Tenochtitlan's Plaza Mayor or main civic precinct.[8] This frieze is now housed in the Aztec room of the National Museum of Anthropology in Mexico City. How many other Toltec treasures lie beneath the streets of Mexico City?

The Aztecs commemorated the greatness of Tula and its god-ruler Quetzalcoatl by carving his image and birthdate in living rock on the face of La Malinche ridge across the river from Tula Grande. Petroglyphs are always difficult to date because they are not associated with other remains, but a careful stylistic analysis of the carving and an adjacent one of Centeotl, the Aztec maize god, has established that they were done during the Late Horizon rather than in Toltec times.[9]

The El Cielito Aztec palace mentioned earlier was built on a flat ridgetop on the other side of the valley. Although only a small portion of it has been excavated, we know that it was constructed in pre-Columbian times and renovated after the Spanish conquest. The evidence for the postconquest occupation includes Tesoro phase pottery with Spanish designs, and European architectural features such as a fireplace and a true keystone arch. A large platform mound on the valley floor beneath El Cielito had been subjected to looting by treasure hunters in the early 1970s, and we found many fragments plate 41 of elaborate imported polychrome pots in the earth they had disturbed. This structure may be a further palace or some other élite building; in any case the two structures suggest that the Late Horizon civic precinct was situated here rather than at Tula Grande.

Sixteenth-century documents also indicate Tula's unusual position in the Aztec world. Sahagun alluded to it in previously cited passages describing the Aztec search for Toltec jewelry, pottery, etc. Other documents studied by Nigel Davies and R.C. Padden show that the Aztecs were interested in more than just pretty objects. Davies cites evidence for several marriages between the ruling dynasties of Tenochtitlan and Tula.[10] These familial ties served to validate and strengthen the claims of the Aztec dynasty to the throne and provide them with an aura of legitimacy. The latest of the marriages united one of Moctezuma's sons and a Tula woman. After the conquest he was christened Don Pedro Tlacahuepan and given the title Duque de Moctezuma de Tultengo. Don Pedro probably lived in the El Cielito palace, and Davies notes that his title is still encountered in those parts. Moctezuma is a common surname in the Tula area to this day, and when I encountered people bearing it I often wondered if they were direct descendants of the Aztec emperor, or perhaps even of the Toltec rulers who built the temples overlooking their homes.

One final point is relevant to Aztec Tula. Documents studied by R.C. Padden show that the Tula area was the final resting place for the most sacred Aztec idol, that of Huitzilopochtli, or Huichilobos as the Spaniards called him.[11] He was the Aztec's tutelary god during their wanderings before they settled down in the Basin of Mexico, and although they quickly adopted many older Mesoamerican deities, they always felt they were Huitzilopochtli's chosen people. Although the Spaniards believed this idol had been destroyed during their savage conquest and destruction of Tenochtitlan, it was in fact taken from the temple and hidden. Faithful Indians who refused to accept the Catholic religion of their conquerors worshipped the idol in secret, moving it from place to place to avoid detection. It became the rallying point for pagan revivalism in the 1540s when Bishop Zumarraga, the highest Church official in 'New Spain', learned of its existence. Despite strenuous efforts, the Bishop and the Inquisition he headed were never able to locate this potential threat to the Colony and the Church. The last thing the Spaniards learned about it was that it was hidden in an unknown cave near Tula, where it may still remain today. What better place to hide such a sacred relic than in the shadow of your civilization's birthplace?

Notes

Bibliography

List of illustrations

Index

Notes

Abbreviations

Am. Ant.   American Antiquity
RMEA   Revista Mexicana de Estudios Antropologicos

Chapter 1

1 Sahagun, b. de 1961, Book Ten 165.
2 Sahagun, B. de 1961, Book Ten, 165.

Chapter 2

1 Sahagun, B. de 1961, Book Ten, 171–72.
2 Sahagun, B. de 1961, Book Ten, 174.
3 Leon-Portillo, M. *Los Antiguos Mexicanos a Traves de sus Cronicas y Cantares*, Mexico DF 1972, 23–24.
4 Santley, R. unpublished ms.
5 Diaz del Castillo, B. *The Discovery and Conquest of Mexico*, New York 1958, 190–91.

Chapter 3

1 Sahagun, B. de 1961, Book Ten, 165.
2 Charnay, D. *The Ancient Cities of the New World*, New York 1973, 75–127.
3 Morley, S. and G. Brainerd, *The Ancient Maya*, 3rd edn, Stanford 1956, 79–99.
4 Gamio, M. *La Poblacion del Valle de Teotihuacan*, 3 vols, Mexico DF 1922.
5 Acosta, J. 1956–57.
6 Armillas, P. 'Teotihuacan, Tula y Los Toltecas: las culturas post-arcaicas y pre-Aztecas del centro de Mexico', *Revista de la Universidad Nacional de Argentina* 3 (1950), 37–70.

Chapter 4

1 Cook, S. 'The historical demography and ecology of the Teotlalpan', *Ibero-Americana* 33 (1949), Los Angeles and Berkeley.
2 Mastache, A.G. in Matos Moctezuma, E. (ed.) 1976, 49–68.
3 Gonzales Quintero, L. *Tipos de vegetacion del Valle del Mexquital, Hgo.*, Mexico DF 1968.
4 Mastache, A.G. and A.M. Crespo, unpublished ms.

5 Diaz, C.L. 'Chingu: un sitio clasico del area de Tula, Hgo.', tesis profesional, Escuela Nacional de Antropologia e Historia, Mexico DF 1978.
6 McBride, H. 'The extent of the Chipicuaro tradition' in *The Natalie Wood Collection of Pre-Columbian Ceramics from Chupicuaro, Guanajuato, Mexico*, Los Angeles 1969, 33–49.
7 Mastache, A.G. and A.M. Crespo, *op. cit.*
8 Davies, C.M.B. 1977, 3–23.
9 Cobean, R. 1978, fig. 4.
10 Yadeun Angulo, J. 1975, 33.
11 Stoutamire, J. 1975, 79.
12 Matos Moctezuma, E. in Matos Moctezuma, E. (ed.), 1974.
13 Davies, C.N.B. 1977, 142–71.
14 Kelley, J.C. 1971.
15 Braniff, B. 'Oscilacion de la frontera septentrional mesoamericana', in Bell, B. (ed.) *The Archaeology of West Mexico*, Ajijic, Jalisco, Mexico 1974, 40–50.
16 Holien, T. and R. Pickering, 'Analogues in Classic period Chalchihuites cultures to late Mesoamerican ceremonialism', in Pasztory, E. (ed.) *Middle Classic Mesoamerica: AD 400–700*. New York and Guildford, Surrey 1978, 145–57.
17 Davies, C.N.B. 1977, 142–50.
18 Sahagun, B. de 1961, Book Ten, 165–66.

Chapter 5

1 Sahagun, B. de 1961, Book Ten, 165.
2 Davies, C.N.B. 1977, 171–75.
3 Jimenez Moreno, W. 'Sintesis de la historia procolonial del Valle de Mexico', *RMEA* XIV (1954–55), 219–36.
4 Yadeun Angulo, J. 1975, 23.
5 Millon, R. 'Teotihuacan: completion of map of giant ancient city in the Valley of Mexico', *Science* 170 (1970), 1077–82.
6 Sahagun, B. de 1961, Book Ten, 166.
7 Acosta, J. 'El enigma de los chacmooles en

Tula', *Estudios Antropologicos en Homenaje al Doctor Manuel Gamio*, Mexico DF 1956, 159–70.
8 Sahugun, B. de 1961, Book Ten, 165–66.

Chapter 7

1 Sahagun, B. de 1952, Book Three, 14.
2 Mastache, A.G. in Matos Moctezuma, E. (ed.) 1976, 64–68.
3 Sahagun, B. de 1961, Book Ten, 168.
4 Sahagun, B. de 1961, Book Ten, 167.
5 Tejera, N., C. 'Tecnologia de una vasija en travertino', *Boletin del Instituto Nacional de Antropologia e Historia* 41 (1970), 48–52.
6 Diehl, R. and E. Stroh Jr. 'Tecali vessel manufacturing debris at Tollan, Mexico', *Amt. Ant.* 43 (1978), 73–79.
7 Mandeville, M. in Diehl, R. (ed.) 1974, 122–29.
8 Sanders, W., J. Parsons, and R. Santley, 1979, 143.
9 Benfer, R.A., personal communication.
10 Hester, T., R. Jack, and A. Benfer, 'Trace element analysis of obsidian from Michoacan, Mexico: preliminary results', *Contributions of the University of California Archaeological Facility* 18 (1973), 167–76.
11 Healan, D. personal communication, 1981.
12 Stocker, T. and M. Spence, in Diehl, R. (ed.) 1974, 88–94.
13 Diaz del Castillo, B. *op cit*, 215–17.

Chapter 8

1 Davies, C.N.B. 1977, 313; Feldman, L. in Diehl, R. (ed.) 1974, 138; Jimenez, Moreno, W. *op cit.*
2 Hirth, K. 1977, 44.
3 Sanders, W.T., J.R. Parsons, and R. Santley, 1979, 1–10.
4 *Ibid.*, 130.
5 Parsons, J. 'An archaeological evaluation of the Codex Xolotl', *Am. Ant.* 35 (1970), 431–40.
6 Charlton, T. 'Tecoco region archaeology and the Codex Xolotl', *Am. Ant.* 38 (1974), 412–23; Blanton, R. 'Texcoco region archaeology: a comment', *Am. Ant.* 40 (1974), 227–30.
7 Muller, F. in Marquina, I. (ed.) 1970, 129–42; Dumond, D. and F. Muller, 'Classic to postClassic in highland central Mexico', *Science* 125 (1972), 1208–15; Mountjoy, J. and D. Peterson, 'Man and land in prehispanic Cholula', *Vanderbilt University Papers in Anthropology* (1973), # 4.
8 Mulloy, J. personal communication 1980.
9 Litvak King, J. 'Xochicalco en la caida del Clasico', *Anales de Antropologia* VII (1970), 131–44; Hirth, K. *op cit*.
10 *Ibid.*
11 Pollard, H.P. 'An analysis of urban zoning and planning at prehispanic Tzintzuntazan', *Proceedings of the American Philosophical Society*, 121 (1977), 46–69; Chadwick, R. in Wauchope, R. (ed.), vol. 11 (1971), 657–93.
12 Piña Chan, R. *Teotenango: el antiguo lugar de la muralla*, Toluca, Mexico 1977.

Chapter 9

1 Blanton, R. 1978.
2 Marcus, J. 'The origins of Mesoamerican writing', *Annual Review of Anthropology* 5 (1976), 35–67.
3 Blanton, R. *op cit*, 96–98; Winter, M. 'Residential patterns at Monte Alban, Oaxaca, Mexico', *Science* 186 (1974), 981–87.
4 Marcus, J. 'Zapotec writing', *Scientific American* 242 (1980), 50–64.
5 Caso, A. in Wauchope, R. (ed.) vol. 3 (1965), 931–47.
6 Chadwick, R. in Wauchope, R. (ed.) (1971), 474–504; Marcus, J. and R. Spores, 'The Handbook of Middle American Indians: a retrospective look', *American Anthropologist* 80 (1978), 85–100.
7 Mulloy, J. personal communication, 1980.
8 Coe, M. in Wauchope, R. (ed.) vol. 3 (1965), 679–715; Santley, R. unpublished ms.
9 Garcia Payon, J. in Wauchope, R. (ed.) vol. 11 (1971), 505–42.
10 *Ibid.*, Table 1.

11 Stresser-Pean, G. in Wauchope, R. (ed.) vol. 11 (1971), 582–602; Diehl, R. and L. Feldman, in Matos Moctezuma, E. (ed.) 1974, 105–08.

12 Stresser-Pean, G., in Wauchope, R. (ed.) vol. 11 (1971), 586–87.

13 Sahagun, B. de, 1952, Book Three, 13–35.

14 Ekholm, G. 'Excavations at Tampico and Panuco in the Huasteca', *Anthropology Papers, American Museum of Natural History* 38 (1944), 319–512; Ochoa, L. *Historia Prehispanica de la Huasteca*, Mexico DF 1979, 72–84.

15 Coe, M. and R. Diehl, *In the Land of the Olmec*, vol. 1, Austin and London 1980, 214.

16 Davies, C.B.N. 1977, 142–50.

17 Culbert, T.P. (ed.) 1973.

18 Willey, G. and D. Shimkin, in *ibid.*, 457–501.

19 Tozzer, A. 'Landa's Relacion de las Cosas de Yucatan', *Peabody Museum Papers*, vol. XVIII (1941).

20 Roys, R. *The Book of Chilam Balam of Chumayel*, Norman 1967.

21 Miller, A., in Hammond, N. (ed.) *Social Process in Maya Prehistory*, London, New York, and San Francisco 1977, 197–225.

22 Andrews IV, E. 'Balankanche, throne of the jaguar priest', *Middle American Research Institute*, Publication 32, New Orleans 1970.

23 Roys, R. *The Book of Chilam Balam of Chumayel* Norman 1967, 177–81.

24 Carmack, R. 'Toltec influence on the PostClassic culture history of highland Guatemala', *Middle American Research Institute*, Publication 26, New Orleans 1968, 49–92; Carmack, R. 1973.

25 Armillas, P. 'The arid frontier of Mexican civilization', *Transactions of the New York Academy of Sciences* N.S. 3 (1969), 697–704: DiPeso, C. 1974, vol. 2; Kelley, J. 1971.

26 Weigand, P., 1978a and b; Weigand, P., G. Harbottle, and E. Sayre, in Earle, T. and J. Ericson (eds.) *Exchange Systems in Prehistory*, New York 1977, 15–34; Weigand, P., 'Mineria y intercambio de minerales en el Zacatecas prehispanica', in *Zacatecas. Anuario de Historia III* (1980), ed. by Cuauhtemoc Esparza Sanchez. Zacatecas, Mexico; Weigand, P. 'Possible references to La Quemada in Huichol myth', *Ethnohistory* 22 (1975), 15–20.

27 Weigand, P. 1978b, 74–78.

28 Weigand, P. 1980 (see note 26 above), 7.

29 Weigand, P. 'The mines and mining techniques of the Chalchihuites culture', *Am. Ant.* 33 (1967), 45–61.

30 Armillas, P. *op cit*.

31 Weigand, P., G. Harbottle, and E. Sayre, *op. cit.*, 22.

32 Weigand, P. 1975 (see note 26 above) 16–17.

33 DiPeso, C. *op cit.*, 701–03.

34 Santley, R. unpublished ms.

Chapter 10

1 Sahagun, B. de 1952, Book Three, 29.

2 Sanders, W. and R. Santley, unpublished ms.

3 Mastache, A.G. in Matos Moctezuma, E. (ed.) 1976, 64–68.

4 Armillas, P. 'Condiciones ambientales y movimientos de pueblos en la frontera septentrional de Mesoamerica', *Homenaje a Fernando Marquez-Miranda*, Madrid and Seville (1964), 62–82.

5 Chadwick, R. in *Wauchope* (ed.) vol. 11 (1971), 677–92.

6 Wolf, E. 1959, ix.

7 Charlton, T. 'Archaeology and History: 1519–1969, The emerging picture in the Teotihuacan Valley, Mexico', *Actas del XLI Congreso Internacional de Americanistas*, Mexico, DF (1975), 225–27.

8 Beyer, H. 'La "Procession de los Senores", decoracion del primer teocalli en piedra de Mexico-Tenochtitlan', *El Mexico Antiguo* 8 (1955), 8–42.

9 Navarrete, C. and A.M. Crespo, 'Un atlante Mexica y algunas consideraciones sobre los relieves del Cerro de la Malinche, Hidalgo', *Estudios de Cultura Nahuatl* IX (1971), 13–15.

10 Davies, C.N.B. 1977, 42.

11 Padden, R. *The Hummingbird and the Hawk: Conquest and Sovereignty in the Valley of Mexico 1503–1541*, New York, Evanston, and London 1967, 240–74.

Bibliography

ACOSTA, Jorge R. 1956–57 'Interpretacion de algunos de los datos obtenidos en Tula relativos a la epoca Tolteca', *Revista Mexicana de Estudios Antropologicos* 14:75–110, Mexico DF.

ADAMS, Richard E. W. 1977 *Prehistoric Mesoamerica*, Boston.

BLANTON, Richard 1978 *Monte Alban: Settlement Patterns at the Ancient Zapotec Capital*, New York.

CARMACK, Robert 1973 *Quichean Civilization: The Ethnohistoric, Ethnographic, and Archaeological Sources*, Berkeley, Los Angeles, and London.

COBEAN, Robert 1978 'The PreAztec Ceramics of Tula, Hidalgo, Mexico', unpublished PhD dissertation, Department of Anthropology, Harvard University.

COE, Michael D. 1977 *Mexico*, 2nd edn, London and New York.

1980 *The Maya*, 2nd edn, London and New York.

CULBERT, T. Patrick (ed.) 1973 *The Classic Maya Collapse*, Albuquerque.

DAVIES, C. Nigel B. 1977 *The Toltecs Until the Fall Of Tula*. Norman.

DIEHL, Richard A. 1981 'Tula', in Sabloff, J. (ed.) *Supplement to the Handbook of Middle American Indians*, vol. 1, Archaeology: 277–95, Austin and London.

DIEHL, Richard A. (ed.) 1974 *Studies of Ancient Tollan: A Report of the University of Missouri Columbia Tula Archaeological Project*. University of Missouri Monographs in Anthropology # 1. Columbia.

DIEHL, Richard A. and Robert A. BENFER 1975 'Tollan, the Toltec Capital', *Archaeology* 28:112–24.

DIPESO, Charles 1974 *Casas Grandes: A Fallen Trading Center in the Gran Chichimeca*, 8 vols, Dragoon, Arizona.

DUTTON, Bertha P. 1955 'Tula of the Toltecs', *El Palacio* LXII: 195–251, Santa Fé.

HEALAN, Dan M. 1974 'Residential Architecture and Household Patterning in Ancient Tula', Unpublished PhD dissertation, Department of Anthropology, University of Missouri, Columbia.

1978 'Architectural implications of daily life in ancient Tollan, Hidalgo, Mexico', *World Archaeology* 9:140–56.

HIRTH, Kenneth 1977 'Toltec Mazapan influence in eastern Morelos, Mexico', *Journal of New World Archaeology* 2(1): 40–46.

KELLEY, J. Charles 1971 'Archaeology of the northern frontier: Zacatecas and Durango', in Wauchope, R. (ed.), vol. 11, 768–801.

MARQUINA, Ignacio (ed.) 1970 'Proyecto Cholula', *Serie Investigaciones* 19, Instituto Nacional de Antropologia e Historia, Mexico DF.

MATOS MOCTEZUMA, Eduardo (ed.) 1974 'Proyecto Tula, primera parte', *Collecion Cientifica* # 15, Instituto Nacional de Antropologia e Historia, Mexico DF.

1976 'Proyecto Tula, segunda parte', *Coleccion Cientifica* # 33, Instituto Nacional de Antropologia e Historia, Mexico DF.

MILLON, René 1973 *Urbanization at Teotihuacan, Mexico*, vol. 1, The *Teotihuacan Map*, Austin and London.

PADDOCK, John (ed.) 1966 *Ancient Oaxaca: Discoveries in Mexican Archaeology and History*, Stanford.

SABLOFF, Jeremy A. (ed.) 1981 *Supplement to the Handbook of Middle American In-*

dians, vol. 1, *Archaeology*, Austin and London.

SAHAGUN, Friar Bernardino de 1950–1969 *Florentine Codex: General History of the Things of New Spain*, 12 vols, translated by Arthur J. O. Anderson and Charles F. Dibble, Santa Fé.

SANDERS, William T., Jeffrey R. PARSONS, and Robert S. SANTLEY 1979 *The Basin of Mexico: Ecological Processes in the Evolution of a Civilization*, New York.

SANDERS, William T. and Barbara J. PRICE 1968 *Mesoamerica: The Evolution of a Civilization*, New York.

STOUTAMIRE, James 1975 'Trend Surface Analysis of Survey Data from Tula, Mexico', Unpublished PhD dissertation, Department of Anthropology, University of Missouri, Columbia.

THOMPSON, Sir J. Eric S. 1966 *The Rise and Fall of the Maya*, 2nd edn, Norman.

WAUCHOPE, Robert (ed.) 1965–75 *Hand-book of Middle American Indians*, vols 1–15, Austin and London.

WEAVER, Muriel Porter 1980 *The Aztecs, Maya, and Their Predecessors: Archaeology of Mesoamerica*, New York and London.

WEIGAND, Phil C. 1978a 'The prehistory of the state of Zacatecas: an interpretation, part 1', *Anthropology, State University of New York, Stony Brook* 2 (1): 67–87.

1978b 'The prehistory of the State of Zacatecas: an interpretation, part 2', *Anthropology, State University of New York, Stony Brook* 2(2): 22–41.

WOLF, Eric 1959 *Sons of the Shaking Earth*, Chicago and London.

1976 (ed.) *The Basin of Mexico: Studies in Pre-Hispanic Ecology and Society*, Albuquerque.

YADEUN Angulo, Juan 1975 'El Estado y La Ciudad: El Caso de Tula, Hgo', *Coleccion Cientifica # 25*, Instituto Nacional de Antropologia e Historia, Mexico DF.

List of illustrations

Unless otherwise acknowledged, the color plates are by Robert Cobean.

Color plates

Monochrome plates

Index

Bold-face numerals refer to text figures;
italic numerals indicate plates